girls

girls

A History of Growing Up Female in America

Penny Colman

SCHOLASTIC NONFICTION

Acknowledgments

As I researched, wrote, revised, and did the picture research and photography for this book, many people participated in various ways, including David Colman, Jonathan Colman, Stephen Colman, Cam Earnest, Linda Estel, Jennifer Fleisher, Anne Foster, Jean Gushkin, Linda Hickson, Maja Keech, Hedy Leutner, Ellen Ochoa, Steven Phelan, Jessy Randall, Charlotte Schoen, Barbara Sheedy, Diane Stallings, Laura Wasowicz, Doris Weatherford, Sarah Weatherwax, Guy Weber, Bridgett Williams-Searle, Dawn Wittman; the editor, Kate Waters; and the art director, Nancy Sabato. Margaret Smith Crocco, Associate Professor of Social Studies and Education, Teachers College, Columbia University, shared her expertise and reviewed the manuscript.

I would also like to thank Harry Walters, Hatathli Museum, Diné College; Mary Degenhardt, Girl Scouts of the U.S.A.; Sharon Lefebvre, Girl Power Headquarters; Kelly Parisi, Ms. Foundation; and Bettye Lane, who generously sent me a selection of her photographs.

I am grateful to the generations of scholars who have written so much wonderful women's history, including Darlene Clark Hine, Linda K. Kerber, Gerda Lerner, Carolyn Niethammer, Vicki Ruiz, Laurel Thatcher Ulrich, and Judy Yung. As for the actual girls and women throughout American history who were able to leave records of their lives, I cherished the opportunity to learn their true stories.

LIBRARY OF CONGRESS CATALOGING-IN-PUBLICATION DATA
Colman, Penny.
Girls: a history of growing up female in America / by Penny Colman.
p. cm.
Includes bibliographical references and index.
Summary: Traces the history of growing up female in America as told by the girls themselves in journals, letters, slave narratives, and other primary sources.
1. Girls—United States—Social conditions Juvenile literature.
2. Teenage girls—United States—Social conditions Juvenile literature.
3. Girls—United States—History Juvenile literature.
4. Teenage girls—United States—History Juvenile literature.
[1. Girls—History.] I. Title.
HQ798.C567 2000 · 305.23'0973—dc21 · 99-28150

ISBN 0-590-37130-4 (pb)

10 9 8 7 6 5 4 3 2 1   03 04 05 06 07
Printed in the U.S.A.
First trade paperback printing, February 2003

Interior design and composition by Nancy Sabato
Interior collages by Paul Colin
Picture research and some photography by Penny Colman
Photographs taken by Penny Colman copyright © 2000 by Penny Colman
All photo credits and text credits appear on pages 191-192.

To Jackie Magness and Liz Roslewicz

For your friendship, laughter, and passion for women's history

Contents

Author's Note

The idea for this book came to me when the words—Girls: A History of Growing Up Female in America—suddenly popped up in my brain like a jack-in-the-box. At the time, I was standing at the corner of Broadway and Twentieth Street in New York City thinking about ordinary things—getting home, cooking dinner, and finishing an article. Now, it is not unusual for words, ideas, and images to spontaneously show up in my brain. Some leave soon, some stay. Some are useful, some are not. Some make me laugh, some depress me. Others inspire me. The words—Girls: A History of Growing Up Female in America—electrified me.

When I started to gather material for this book, I looked for information about girls' lives in many places, including advice books, magazines, official documents, paintings, photographs, advertisements, lyrics, and novels. I visited museums, archives, libraries, and historic sites. I talked with historians and read scholarly materials on a variety of subjects, including childhood, women's history, toys, and work. In addition, I asked people what they wanted to know about growing up female in America. The answers I got ranged from "anything and everything!" to questions such as: What sports did girls play? What kind of books did girls read? What was considered appropriate behavior for girls?

It was not easy to find information, because the experiences of girls were rarely recorded. In addition, most girls themselves did not have the opportunity to leave a record of what they did and thought. Some girls, however, did leave a record.

On May 25, 1772, twelve-year-old Anna Green Winslow wrote in her journal about trying out the popular hairstyle of elevating her hair by wearing a small cushion called a roll on her head. A roll frequently weighed fourteen ounces, and it was considered very fashionable. According to Anna, "It makes my head itch, & ach, & burn like anything. . . . This famous roll is not made *wholly* of a red *Cow Tail*, but is a mixture of that, & horsehair (very coarse) & a little human hair of yellow hue, that I suppose was taken out of the back part of an old wig."

Anna Green Winslow

On November 21, 1852, Caroline Cowles Richards wrote, "I am ten years old to-day, and I think I will write a journal and tell who I am and what I am doing."

On December 15, 1926, fourteen-year-old Yvonne Blue wrote in her diary: "Bobbie and I are going to be wonderful. . . . Our new passion is self-improvement. I stayed all night at her house last night and we made up a wonderful set of rules. We each have a little blue-covered notebook, and we wrote the rules in India Ink on the cover,

> Keep polished.
> Follow the Health Chart.
> Talk the right amount and clearly.
> Be adventurous and light.
> Be decisive and 'stick to your guns.'
> Go to extremes
> Train Mind
> Be noble—in a princess way
> Have a way with people.

"We are going to take one each day and concentrate on it alone. Today we took the first. If we are good for a week we have a little spree—a movie and a sundae together, but if we have a blank space for *one day* we have the most horrible punishment in the world—doing the dishes for that night."

Girls who had the opportunity also wrote letters. While she was away at school, twelve-year-old Eliza Southgate wrote letters to her family and friends. On January 23, 1797, she wrote to her mother, "My Mamma, . . . I have a great desire to see my family, but I have a still greater desire to finish my education. . . . Still I have to beg you to remind my friends and acquaintances that I remain the same Eliza, and that I bear the same love I ever did to them, whether they have forgotten me or not. . . . Permit me, my Honored Mother, to claim the title of Your affectionate daughter, Eliza Southgate."

Two friends in Boston, Ednah Dow Littlehale and Caroline Wells Healy, wrote letters to each other. In 1838, when Ednah was thirteen years old, she wrote to Caroline, "What do I mean by the rights of women!!! *mean*, I mean what I say—we have as good a right to rule men as they have to rule us." To which Caroline, who was fifteen years old, replied, "I do not deny that women may have the right to vote; the right to legislation . . . but what *lady* would claim the right?"

Other girls were women, oftentimes older women, when they created accounts—oral testimonies, memoirs, and autobiographies—of their girlhood.

Joanna Draper remembered her experience as a slave during the years just before the Civil War. "When I is about six years old, they take me into the big house to learn to be a house woman, and they show me how to cook and clean up and take care of babies."

Buffalo Bird Woman, whose real name was Maxidiwiac, reminisced about growing up in the 1840s and eating breakfast in the field where the women in her family grew crops. "Our food we had brought with us, usually buffalo meat, fresh or dried. Fresh meat we laid on the coals to broil. Dried meat we thrust on a stick and held over the fire to toast. Sometimes we brought a clay cooking pot, and boiled squashes. We were fond of squashes and ate many of them. We sometimes boiled green corn and beans. My sister and I shelled the corn from the cob. We shelled the beans or boiled them in the pod. My grandmother poured the mess in a wooden bowl, and we ate with spoons which she made from squash stems. She would split a stem with her knife and put in a little stick to hold the split open. I do not think anything can taste sweeter than a mess of fresh corn and beans, in the cool morning air, when the birds are twittering and the sun is just peeping over the tree tops."

Sharlot Hall

Sharlot Hall recalled her journey to Arizona when she was eleven years old: "My parents moved from Barbour County, Kansas . . . to Yavapai County, Arizona. We started on the third day of November [1881] with two covered wagons drawn by four horses each. I rode a little Texas pony and drove a band of horses. We followed the old Sante Fe trail nearly all the way."

Andreita Padilla recalled her girlhood in the early 1920s growing up in New Mexico. "Sometimes when we finished all the work, I'd play with my friends. We'd jump rope, play hopscotch and sing and dance to 'Naranja Dulce.' We sang it like this:

Naranja dulce,	Sweet orange,
Limon partido,	Halved lemon,
Dame un abrazo,	Give me a hug,
Que yo te pido.	Because I'm asking you.

It was so pretty."

Another source of information was mothers' and fathers' accounts about their daughters. These accounts included descriptions of the types of clothes parents bought for their daughters, the expectations they had for their daughters, and their daughters' daily activities.

In a letter Benjamin Franklin wrote to his mother in 1750, he provided a glimpse of both his expectations and his daughter Sally's activities: "Sally grows a fine Girl, and is extreamly industrious with her Needle, and delights in her Book. She is of a most affectionate Temper, and perfectly dutiful and obliging to her Parents, and to all. Perhaps I flatter myself too much, but I have hopes that she will prove an ingenious, sensible, notable, and worthy Woman, like her Aunt Jenny. She goes now to the Dancing-School."

In 1760, George Washington wrote a letter to a firm in London, England, with an order for outfits for his four-year-old stepdaughter, including pack-thread stays, stiff coats of silk, caps, bonnets, bibs, ruffles, necklaces, fans, silk and calamanco shoes, eight pairs of kid mitts and four pairs of gloves.

Abigail Adams wrote in 1777 about her twelve-year-old daughter Abigail, who was called Nabby, "I am happy in a daughter who is both a companion and an assistant in my Family affairs and who I think has a prudence and steadiness beyond her years."

Emmeline Wells, the mother of five daughters, wrote in about 1868, "I am determined to train my girls to habits of independence so that they have sufficient energy of purpose to carry out plans for their own welfare and happiness."

I wrote this book because the fact of being born female in America matters, and it always has. For most of American history, it meant fewer rights, freedoms, and opportunities. It meant stereotypes, jokes, and teasing. Nevertheless, many girls faced growing up female with vigor.

Countless numbers of girls confronted their fears, overcame obstacles, spoke their minds, cherished their friends and family, contributed to the world around them, and left a legacy that can educate and inspire girls in other times and places.

The story about growing up female in America is not one girl's story but many girls'—Native American; colonial; slave; immigrant; pioneer; rich, middle-class, and poor. It is the stirring story of ordinary and extra-ordinary girls who found ingenious ways of making do and performed incredible feats of derring-do.

I

"It's a Girl!"

UNDERSTANDING GENDER

From the moment a newborn baby's sex is announced—"It's a girl!" or "It's a boy!"—girls and boys are perceived and treated differently. This has been true throughout history. In all times and places, societies have had definitions of female and male traits, abilities, and roles. The definitions, known as gender roles, evolve and change, but they never disappear. There are many opinions about why gender roles developed. Some people think gender roles originated as a way to divide up work. Other people think gender roles evolved from the fact that women give birth and men do not. Then there are people who think that gender roles are simply innate, or present at birth.

In Western societies, the female gender role is usually described as nurturing, expressive, cooperative, and sensitive to the needs of others. The male gender role is usually described as independent, aggressive, dominant, and ambitious. Gender roles are reflected in many ways. One interesting study done in 1993 describes how gender roles are expressed in greeting cards that people send to congratulate parents on a new baby. Cards for baby girls have toys, rattles, and mobiles. Boys' cards have balls, sports equipment, and vehicles. Boys' cards are never pink. Girls' cards are never blue. In addition, girls' cards typically have frills, lace, ribbons, flowers, and hearts. Boys are shown more often in active play. Girls are usually shown sleeping or in a still position. The word "sweet" is used far more often for girls than boys.

From an early age, Elizabeth Cady Stanton was aware that people had different ideas about girls and boys. "The first event engraved on my memory was the birth of a sister when I was four years old," Stanton recalled. "It was a cold morning in January [1819] when the brawny Scotch nurse carried me to see the little stranger, whose advent was a matter of intense interest to me for many weeks after. The large, pleasant room with the white curtains and bright wood fire on the hearth, . . . was the center of attraction for the older children. I heard so many friends remark, 'What a pity it is she's a girl!' that I felt a kind of compassion for the little baby. True, our family consisted of five girls and only one boy but I did not understand at the time that girls were considered an inferior order of being."

Elizabeth's brother died when she was eleven. "A young man of great talent and promise, he was the pride of my father's heart," she later wrote. While Elizabeth was trying to console her father, he told her, "I wish you were a boy." To which she replied, "I will try to be all my brother was." According to Elizabeth, she "pondered the problem of boyhood" and decided that the "chief thing to be done in order to

In the past, many schools had separate doors for girls and boys.
The separation is illustrated in this picture of a fire drill from an 1889 newspaper.

equal boys was to study Greek and learn to manage a horse."

Elizabeth worked hard. "I surprised even my teacher [Greek], who thought me capable of doing anything," she recalled. "I learned to drive, and to leap a fence and ditch on horseback. I taxed every power, hoping some day to hear my father say: 'Well, a girl is as good as a boy, after all.' But he never said it."

The history of growing up female has many accounts that record adults expressing strong ideas to girls about what it meant to be a girl. Buffalo Bird Woman remembered that when she dressed up in her father's hunting cap, her grandmother always said, "That is a warrior's cap. A little girl can not be a warrior." In her autobiography, Rosalie Slaughter related her father's response when she told him that she wanted to be a doctor. "'I do not want my daughter to earn money,' he said firmly, '. . . your highest duty is to become a good wife and mother.'"

Hilda Satt Polacheck recalled, "I have been told that there was great consternation in the family when I was born. There were no boys in the family at the time, and I was the fourth daughter to arrive. While daughters were tolerated, it was important to have sons in the family, so that they would recite the Kaddish (the mourners' prayer for their parents after their death). The recital of the Kaddish by a daughter was not acceptable."

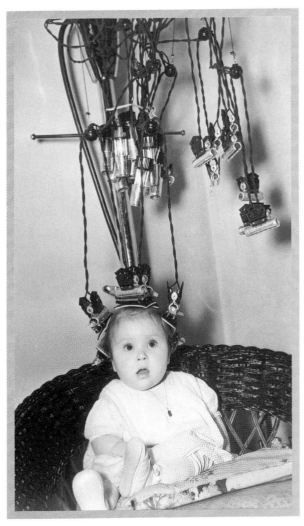

A baby girl in 1938 getting a permanent wave to curl her hair. The wires heated clamps that were put on each curler.

These attitudes did not necessarily mean that girls were loved less than boys. Gender roles were not necessarily intended to favor one sex over the other. However, boys typically grew up with a great deal of freedom and many opportunities. Girls, on the other hand, often encountered limitations of their freedoms and opportunities.

In 1856, Frances Willard wrote in her diary, "Mother insists that at last I must have my hair 'done up woman-fashion.' She says she can hardly forgive herself for letting me 'run wild' so long. We've had a great time over it all. . . . My 'back' hair is twisted up like a corkscrew: I carry eigh-teen hair-pins; my head aches miserably; my feet are entangled in the skirt of my hateful new gown. I can never jump over a fence again, so long as I live. As for chasing the sheep, down in the shady pasture, it's out of the question."

Joanna Carver Colcord recalled growing up in the 1880s, when she and her brother had a "sea upbringing" on board her father's sailing ship: "My brother was early allowed to climb aloft, but this joy was always denied to me; and as I got older my range on deck was restricted more than his—I might not go forward of the mainmast, and I must always behave qui-etly, like a little lady. Also I had to learn to sew and he did not. Tomboy that I was, all this irked me deeply, but I toed the mark."

Betsy Miller, who was born in 1929, recalled how she learned about gender roles. "I was a great runner. I would run all the way to school every day and back, and I bicycled a lot. I was a tall child, so I stopped in the morning to play basketball with the other boys before school. I was never allowed to play real football, but I played sandlot football and sandlot baseball and sandlot basketball. . . . If I had been a boy, I would imagine someone would have said, ' . . . you could be a triathlon athlete.' Also, 'You're very good at math.'"

"As time went on, I saw the other girls were more oriented towards the female role, so I had to move over. I had to stop playing [sports] and I had to be my sex and play my role in society. I started to stop doing those things when I developed breasts. I couldn't get out there in a T-shirt and jeans and look like a little boy anymore. I was a female, and I was destined to marry and have a family. My family was trying to mold me into the proper debutante type, so I worked very hard at being that. I put on my little suit and gloves and hat and went

A dance at the Cotton Carnival in Memphis, Tennessee, in 1940.

to more of the social things. When we were fourteen years old, we went to lots of charity tea parties and dances."

Mary Wong Leong recalled what life was like for the children in her family as they worked in the family laundry business. "My sister and I would help load up the trucks . . . go to all these different laundries and drop off the clean laundry and carry out all the dirty laundry. . . . Many times we girls worked till like one and two in the morning sorting a mountain of laundry. The boys didn't have to do that. They became delivery drivers, and when they were done with delivery, they were free. . . . They were paid five dollars a delivery—we were paid twenty-five cents a delivery."

Gender roles in one form or another have existed throughout American history. Some girls have accepted them. Some girls have been stymied by them. Other girls have found ways to go around, over, and under them. Other girls have challenged them head-on. But every girl has had to deal with gender roles because they have been—and still are—reflected everywhere, in stories and novels, advice books, toys and games, clothing, advertisements, music, movies, radio, and television.

2

By Land and By Sea

HOW GIRLS CAME TO AMERICA

The first girls walked to America. They came during the last stages of the Ice Age with small bands of people now called Paleo-Indians. The route they most likely took led from Asia across a land bridge that is now covered by the Bering Sea. The Paleo-Indians gathered seeds, roots, and fruit and hunted big animals—giant bison, woolly mammoths, caribou, and beavers the size of grizzly bears. In time, the Paleo-Indians migrated throughout what today is known as North and South America, from the Arctic to the southernmost tip of South America. Over many millennia, the descendants of the Paleo-Indians figured out how to survive in a great variety of environments—forests, deserts, mountains, canyons, coastlines, lakeshores, river valleys, and grassy plains. They devised weapons, tools, and pottery; discovered

Many experts believe that during the Ice Age Asia and North America were connected by the land bridge, the light area on this map.

new skills and techniques for gaining food and shelter; utilized natural substances for healing; and created communities.

By the time Christopher Columbus sailed in 1492, millions of Native Americans—women and men, boys and girls—already lived on the land that would become known as the New World. These people, whom Columbus called Indians, spoke many different languages and belonged to many distinct tribes and villages. Many Indians were farmers, others lived as hunters and gatherers, and in coastal regions the Indians turned to the ocean and rivers for their livelihood.

Lenape girls lived in a region called Lenapehoking—"Land of the Lenapes"—a region that stretched from the New York Bay to the Delaware Bay. All Lenapes belonged to their mothers' clans, or groups of related families. They lived in round wigwams or longhouses covered with bark or grass. During the summer, little girls wore very little clothing. Older girls wore a simple dress made of cloth that was generally red, blue, or black. In the winter, they wore a blanket made of beaver or raccoon skins. If it was cold and dry, the fur was worn next to the body. If it was warm and wet, the fur was on the outside. Shoes were made of dressed bearskin with the hair on the inside. To protect themselves from the sun in the summer and the cold in the winter, many Lenapes used a lotion made from bears' grease, sunflower oil, or nut oil. During the day, a girl would tend a pot or kettle and cut and fetch firewood. She would help her mother till the soil, sow and reap grain, pound corn in a stamping trough or mortar, weave grasses and reeds into mats and baskets, and make bread that was baked in ashes.

Early Native American people passed on the history, morals, and beliefs of their cultures by telling stories, myths, and legends. They also painted, carved, and wove symbols and images into various objects such as pottery and rugs. A Navajo Creation Story that explained the beginning of the universe and of human beings told about a baby girl. In the story, First Man found the baby girl at the top of Spruce Mountain. He took her home to Mountain-Around-Which-Moving-Was-Done, where he lived with First Woman. The baby girl grew to be a woman. The gods gave her a sacred ceremony, a Blessing Way, Walking-Into-Beauty, to celebrate her becoming a woman. Each day of the ceremony, there were songs and chants. The ceremony is still given today to Navajo girls when they become women.

In time, the woman was called Changing Woman because each winter she became withered and white-haired. But in the spring, she looked young again. When the sun fell in love with Changing Woman, she asked First Woman what she should do. First Woman said Changing Woman should have children with the sun. Changing Woman had twin sons who grew up to fight the monsters that had appeared in the world. The sons finally destroyed the monsters, but not before most of the people had been killed. Changing Woman decided that the world needed more people, so she took a basket of white corn and a basket of yellow corn and ground it. From the white cornmeal, Changing Woman shaped a man. She shaped a woman from the yellow cornmeal.

A 1609 handbill advertising a voyage to Virginia.

She taught humans how to live in harmony with nature. She built the first hogan out of turquoise and shells. She gave the gift of corn. Of all the Navajo Holy People, Changing Woman is always benevolent.

In the 1500s, Europeans started to build colonies in the Native American's world. The Spanish, French, and English made successful and unsuccessful attempts. In 1542, the French established a colony on Parris Island, off the coast of South Carolina, that failed. In 1565, the Spanish established the fort of Saint Augustine in Florida, which became the oldest permanent European city in North America. By 1580, the colonists had built about thirty houses made of wood and mud covered with the lime of oyster shells. Sixty other houses were made of lime and sand and had flat roofs.

In 1598, Juan de Oñate led a group of men, women, and children north from Mexico and established the first Spanish colony in what is now New Mexico. They traveled with sixty-two two-wheeled wood carts filled with household goods and ammunition, and 7,000 animals—oxen, cattle, sheep, goats, mules, and horses. According to one account, "The march began mid a deafening screeching of the cart wheels and the applause of all."

On August 18, 1587, the first baby of English parents was born in the New World. It was a girl. The girl's parents were members of a group of colonists who had sailed from Plymouth, England. They had planned to land in Chesapeake Bay but instead landed on Roanoke Island in Virginia (now part of North Carolina). The girl's mother, Elenor White Dare, was the daughter of John White, who was the governor of the new colony. In his journal, White noted his granddaughter's birth, her christening on August 24, and wrote that "because this childe was the first Christian borne in Virginia, she was named Virginia."

A chief's young daughter (a detail of a watercolor by John White, 1585). The doll in her hand was brought by European colonists. Older girls wore deerskin aprons.

Shortly after Virginia's birth, John White sailed for England to get more supplies. His return was delayed because of a war with Spain. Finally, in 1590, White returned to Roanoke Island. All he found there were ruins. Although there have been many theories about what happened to Virginia Dare, her parents, and the other colonists, no one

The indenture agreement for Mary Elizabeth Bauer. In exchange for her "passage from Holland," Mary was bound to Master Samuel Pleasant for five years.

knows for sure. Over the years, the colony became known as the Lost Colony. Virginia Dare is the subject of art, poetry, drama, and novels, and her name frequently appears in history books.

The hardships and dangers of colonizing the New World did not deter Europeans who were propelled by strong motives. The hope of discovering great riches drove some people. Other people were fleeing something—religious persecution, poverty, famine, political unrest, criminal records, unbearable family situations, and a scarcity of opportunities. Some people were looking for adventure. Whatever their reasons, during the 1600s increasing numbers of Europeans boarded tiny, crowded, and oftentimes leaking ships bound for America. Girls were on board those ships, too. On one voyage from England to Massachusetts, twenty-one girls who were under the age of fifteen were among the

106 passengers. According to the passenger list, the girls included the five daughters of Joseph and Agnes Hull: Joan, "aged 15 years"; Temperance, "aged 9 years"; Elizabeth, "aged 7 years"; Grissel, "aged 5 years"; and Dorothy, "aged 3 years."

Like the Hull girls, most of the girls who came to one of the New England or middle colonies came with their families. Girls who came to the Chesapeake Bay colonies of Maryland and Virginia, however, generally came alone. Some of these girls were orphans or abandoned children in London, England, who were rounded up by agents, known as "spirits." Court records reveal that some spirits were guilty of kidnapping children. The spirits worked for merchants or shipowners who offered the children passage in exchange for an agreement to work for a certain period of time, usually four to seven years. This agreement, known as an indenture, could be sold or assigned to someone else, and merchants and shipowners made money selling them to colonists who were in desperate need of cheap labor.

In the 1600s, the need for labor was so great in Virginia that plantation owners petitioned the city officials in London, England, for "children out of their superfluous multitude to be transported to Virginia." In 1619, the officials of Virginia thanked the "mayor, aldermen, and council of the City of London" for "furnishing one hundred children this last year, which by the goodness of God there safely arrived (save such as died in the way)" and requested one hundred more children "of twelve years old and upward" for the next spring. The officials of London declared that they deserved praise "for redeeming so many poor souls from misery and ruin and putting them in a condition of use and service." If children resisted, the agents were authorized "to imprison, punish, and dispose any of those children . . . and so ship them out for Virginia."

According to court records, girls who were sent to Virginia included Suzan Hutchinson, Hester Wheeler, Jane Morgan, and Prudence Nation. Once a girl arrived in Virginia, her days would be filled with work. Her master would assign her any number of tasks—tending the garden, milking the cow, feeding the pigs, collecting eggs, baking, cooking, sewing, or making candles or soap.

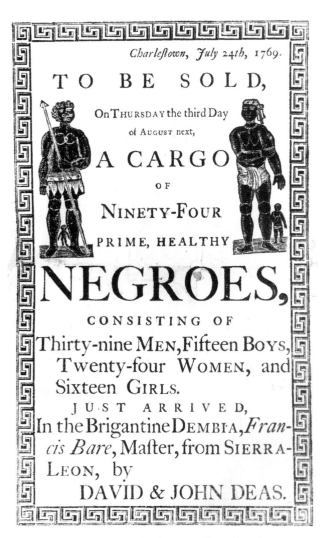

A 1769 broadside advertising slaves for sale, including sixteen girls.

The desire for cheap labor made some colonists eager for African slaves. The plantation owners needed workers to cultivate rice, tobacco, indigo, and later, cotton. Shipbuilders needed workers. Merchants made money selling Africans. The first twenty Africans arrived in Virginia on board a Dutch ship in 1619. They were most likely sold as indentured servants, which was the practice in the early days of the slave trade. In the 1660s, however, laws were passed in Maryland and Virginia that required "all Negroes or other slaves" to serve for the "term of their lives."

Although slave ships carried mostly men and women, boys and girls were there, too. In 1746, William Ellery, a merchant in

Newport, Rhode Island, instructed Captain Pollipus Hammond: "You being Master of our Sloop Anstis and ready to sail, our orders are that you . . . make the best of your way for the Coast of Africa . . . dispose of our Cargoe to the best advantage, make us returns in Negroes. . . . Get most of them mere Boys and Girls, some Men, let them be young, No very small Children." In 1752, in Boston, Massachusetts, a newspaper advertisement announced the arrival of a ship "with a Quantity of very likely Boys and Girls of the blackest Sort." On June 30, 1756, Elias Ball, a planta-

tion owner in South Carolina, recorded information in his journal about slaves he purchased from the captain of the slave ship, *Hare*: "I bought 4 boys & 2 girls—their ages as near I can judge: Sancho— 9 years old, Peter—7, Brutus—7, Harry—6, Belinda—10, Priscilla—10."

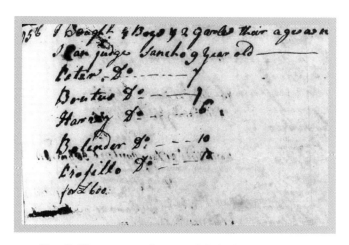

Elias Ball's notation in his journal. Belinda is on line six. Priscilla is on line seven.

During the 1600s and 1700s, most girls came to the east coast of the New World. However, girls did arrive in other parts. In 1704, twenty or more teenage girls and young women, who were French orphans and peasants, landed at Ship Island, Mississippi, as prospective wives for Frenchmen in Louisiana. The girls were known as "Casket Girls" because each girl had a chest or "casquette" containing a trousseau provided by the French government. Eighty more "Casket Girls" arrived in 1721. The French government had asked a bishop to select this group of girls. His choices were dutiful girls who were poor but had some education. Under the supervision of Sisters Gertrude, Louise, and Bergers, the girls arrived aboard the *La Baline* and soon became wives.

In 1769, Spanish and Mexican girls were part of the first overland expedition to reach San Diego, Alta—or Upper—California. Some thirty years later, seven-year-old Apolinaria Lorenzana and her mother arrived in Monterey, Alta California, aboard the *Concepción*. Along with other widows and orphans, they had been sent by the Spanish colonial government in Mexico as potential wives for the soldiers in the presidio (fort). They were also expected to work for the priests in the mission. "Upon our arrival in Monterey," Apolinaria later recalled, "the governor distributed some of the children like puppies. . . . I remained with my mother and various other women. Those [girls] that were already women [had started menstruation], Francisca and Pascuala, were married very soon."

What was life like for the girls who came to America by land and by sea? What did it take to survive? What did it take to thrive?

3

In Their Mothers' Footsteps

GIRLS IN THE EARLY COLONIAL PERIOD

Anne Burras was about thirteen years old and the maid to Mistress Forest, the wife of Thomas, when she arrived in Jamestown, Virginia, aboard the *Mary Margrett* in the fall of 1608. Shortly after her arrival, Anne married John Laydon. It was the first wedding in Jamestown. A year later Anne gave birth to a girl who was named Virginia.

Jamestown had been founded the year before Burras arrived by about one hundred men, including John Laydon, who arrived on board the *Susan Constant*. The London Company, a group of men in England who financed the colony, knew that male colonists could not cook, make clothing, and do the many complex tasks involved in setting up permanent households. Women could, however, and the company recruited them.

An illustration done in the 1800s shows the arrival of a group of potential wives in Jamestown in the 1600s.

At first, the company offered women free land. However, the offer was withdrawn when it became clear that women with land were less likely to get married. The London Company believed that marriage would make the men stay longer in Virginia. In addition, the birth of children would increase the population. According to company records, "Women, Maids young and uncorrupt [were sent] to make Wyves to the Inhabitants and by that means to make the men there more settled & less moveable. . . . Planters' minds may be the faster tied to Virginia by the bonds of Wyves and children." Seven ships arrived in 1609 with one hundred more young women. Later ships brought more young women, some of whom had been kidnapped. Other women who had been convicted of various crimes had been given the choice of prison in England or a voyage to Jamestown. These women were known as "tobacco brides" because men bought them by paying for their passage with tobacco leaves.

Almost a year before Anne Burras arrived, an Indian girl—Matoaka, whose nickname was Pocahontas—had rescued Captain John Smith, who was the military commander of Jamestown. At least that was what Smith later wrote, although no one knows for sure. According to Smith's account, "Two great stones were brought before Powhatan; then as many as could layd hands on him [Smith], dragged him to them and thereon laid his head. . . . [The braves] being ready with their clubs to beate out his braines, Pocahontas, the King's dearest daughter . . . got his head in her arms, and laid her owne upon his to save him from death."

Pocahontas was the daughter of Chief Powhatan. She was about twelve years old when the first colonists arrived. Powhatan was the ruler of the more than two hundred Native American tribes that were living in the area where the English settled. At first Powhatan was friendly toward the English. He became less friendly as some colonists continually stole the Indians' food and encroached on their land. In 1613, the English wanted to force Powhatan to return weapons and Englishmen he had captured, so they kidnapped Pocahontas. After a year in captivity, Pocahontas married a

An illustration from a book about Pocahontas published in 1816. It shows her going to save John Smith for a second time by warning him about her father's plan to attack.

colonist named John Rolfe. After her marriage, Pocahontas converted to Christianity, took the name Rebecca, and wore English clothes. In 1616, she and John went to England, where she had a baby. However, within a year she got sick and died.

Before Pocahontas's death, John Smith wrote a book about America with no mention of Pocahontas at all. But after her death, he revised his book and included the story about how she saved his life. Perhaps because Pocahontas was so dramatically portrayed helping a white man, she has become one of the best-known girls in American history.

Life was extraordinarily difficult in Virginia for the early colonists. Their troubles were seemingly endless—dysentery, fire, drought, Indian attacks, and their own quarrels and rivalries. During the winter of 1609–1610, known as the "starving time," some colonists turned to cannibalism. Out of a population of 550 people, only sixty-five survived, including Anne, Virginia, and John Laydon.

In time, the colony got stronger and began to thrive. A census in 1624 shows that Anne and John had three more girls—Alice, Katherin, and Margerett. The Laydons' names appear in various records that list property dealings through the 1640s. After that point, the fate of any of them is unknown.

In 1620, another group of colonists, who became known as Pilgrims, founded the second permanent English settlement at Plymouth. With this group of colonists were girls named Mary and Ellen Moore, Damaris and Constance Hopkins, Mary and Remember Allerton, Desire Minter, Humility Cooper, Elizabeth Tilley, Mary Chilton, and Priscilla Mullins. Almost half of the Pilgrims died of starvation and disease the first winter, including Mary and Ellen Moore. A few years later, Damaris Hopkins died. Humility Cooper and Desire Minter eventually returned to England. The other girls grew up, got married, and had children—lots of children, as was typical at that time.

Priscilla Mullins made it into the history books because her courtship with John Alden was memorialized by a famous poem that was written long after the event. Priscilla and John were the first people who had not been married before to get married in Plymouth. They had eleven children, including six girls—Elizabeth, Rebecca, Ruth, Sarah, Mary, and Priscilla. Elizabeth Tilley married John Howland and had ten children, including six girls—Desire, Hope, Elizabeth, Lydia, Hannah, and Ruth. Mary Chilton married John Winslow and had three daughters—Susanna, Sarah, and Mary. Constance Hopkins married Nicholas Snow and they moved to Cape Cod. As was common, they gave their daughters names from the Bible—Mary, Sarah, Ruth, and

A statue of Anne Hutchinson and one of her six daughters. In 1638, Hutchinson was banished from the Massachusetts Bay Colony for expressing her religious ideas.

Elizabeth. Remember Allerton married Moses Maverick and moved to Salem and had six daughters—Rebecca, Mary, Abigail, two Elizabeths, and Remember. There were two Elizabeths because the first one died at a young age, and it was the custom when a girl or boy died to pass their name on to the next baby. Mary Allerton, who eventually was the last of the original Pilgrims to die, married Thomas Cushman. They had eight children, including four girls—Sarah, Lydia, Mary, and Fear.

The Pilgrims were part of a larger group of religious people known as Puritans. Ten years after the Pilgrims arrived, a group of Puritans founded the Massachusetts Bay Colony. A year later, they moved to a peninsula that the Indians called Shawmut, and founded Boston. The Puritans' beliefs dominated the religious, legal, and social life of most of the people in the New England colonies. In terms of family life, the Puritans believed that the man was the head, next came the woman, then the children, and finally the servants. Puritans believed that this order was ordained by God and that it was essential to the health of the rest of society. As Cotton Mather, a powerful Puritan minister, put it, "Well-Ordered Families naturally produce a Good Order in other Societies." Another Puritan minister, Benjamin Wadsworth, explained, "The husband is called the head of the woman. It belongs to the head to rule and govern. Wives are part of the house and family, and ought to be under the husband's government."

A painting of Alice Mason, a Puritan girl.

The early Puritans also believed in the doctrine of infant depravity, or the belief that children were born with the inclination to do evil because they were ignorant of what was good. The parents' job, therefore, was to train their children to be obedient and submissive. The first step in that training was to break the child's will. Today some of the measures used by Puritan parents would be considered child abuse, but in colonial times, the harsh treatment was justified as necessary to save a child's soul from the devil. These harsh measures were applied to both girls and boys. "I had almost forgot to tell you that I have begun to govourn Sally," Esther Edwards Burr wrote to her close friend Sarah Prince. "She has been Whip'd once on *Old Adams* [the first man in the Bible] account, and she knows the difference between a smile and a frown as well as I do. When she has done any thing that she suspects is wrong, will look with concern to see what Mama says, and if I only knit my brow she will cry till I smile, and altho' she is not quite Ten months old. Yet when she knows so much, I think tis time she should be taught."

By 1691, all of the thirteen original colonies, with the exception of Georgia, had been settled. There were the New England colonies—Massachusetts, New Hampshire, Connecticut, Rhode Island; the mid-Atlantic colonies—New York, New Jersey, Delaware, and Pennsylvania; the Chesapeake colonies—Virginia and Maryland; and lower South colonies—North Carolina and South Carolina. Georgia was founded in 1732. All the colonies belonged to Great Britain, also called England.

There were vast differences among the colonies. Although the majority of white people were English, there were also French, Dutch, Scotch-Irish, Swedes, Finns, and Germans. The people spoke different languages and practiced different customs and religions. They built different kinds of houses. They wore different types of clothing. They grew

The birth certificate for Anna Barbara Schwarin.
It is a piece of fraktur art, a decorative calligraphy developed by German-speaking people in Pennsylvania.

different crops to sell: wheat and other grains in the mid-Atlantic colonies, tobacco in the Chesapeake colonies, and rice and indigo in the lower South colonies. But despite their differences, all of the colonists agreed on one thing—girls should follow in their mothers' footsteps and grow up to be wives and mothers. Exactly what kind of wife and mother a girl would learn to be varied according to the girl's race, ethnicity, religion, wealth, and geographical location.

Girls who lived on farms, and most did during colonial times, learned how to perform an impressive array of essential tasks. According to Abigail Foote's diary, in one day she: "Fix'd gown for Prude,—Mend Mother's Riding-hood, Spun short thread,—Fix'd two gowns for Welsh's girls,—Carded tow,—Spun linen,—Worked on Cheese-basket,—Hatchel'd flax with Hannah, we did 51 lbs. apiece,—Pleated and ironed, . . . —Spooled a piece,—Milked the Cows,—Spun linen, did 50 knots,—Made a Broom of Guinea wheat straw,—Spun thread to whiten,—Set a Red dye, . . . I carded two pounds of whole wool and felt,—Spun harness twine,—Scoured the pewter, . . . spun thread to whiten. . . . " Abigail, who grew up in Colchester, Connecticut, also wrote about cooking soup, dipping candles, and visiting friends.

By the age of four or five, a girl was helping her mother in the garden—poking seeds into the ground, chasing away crows, and picking Indian corn, peas, beans, and spinach. Inside what was typically a one-room house with a huge fireplace, a girl learned about cooking, baking, and preserving food. Tasks that would baffle most modern cooks were second nature for colonial girls: how to broach (put on a spit) a piece of meat, to sour milk to make cheese, to use a boulter (sifter) or

A drawing of the kitchen in a colonial home. Typically called the hall, it was the center of activity.

pipkins (saucepans), and to prepare forced (scrambled) eggs, a sallat (salad), and pompions (pumpkins). She learned how to use herbs to season foods, heal sicknesses, and chase away nightmares.

Colonial girls learned how to spin thread and weave cloth. Hannah Hickok Smith, the mother of five daughters, described her girls' efforts in a letter to their grandmother: "The girls—have been very busy spinning and have spun enough for about seventy yards besides almost enough for another carpet." Girls also learned how to sew many different stitches. By the age of five or six, a girl had most likely made her first sampler by embroidering a simple rhyme, or the alphabet, or numerals onto a piece of cloth. At the age of eight, Hannah Fisher, a Quaker girl in Philadelphia, Pennsylvania, made her first shirt.

Fifteen-year-old Elizabeth Pecker made this sampler in 1750. She used many different stitches and put a lock of real red-gray hair upon the damsel's head (lower left corner).

If the family had geese, girls learned goose-picking, or how to get the feathers from a live goose. Until the early 1800s, quill pens were used for writing. Most colonial girls, however, rarely used pens because they received very little education in anything other than "housewifery." Girls whose parents knew how to read or write might learn those skills at home. In 1647, Massachusetts passed a law that required every town with at least fifty families to establish an elementary school. Secondary schools, called grammar schools, were to be established in larger towns. While girls could attend elementary schools, where they learned the alphabet, spelling, writing, and basic arithmetic, they could not attend grammar schools.

Well-to-do white girls who lived in a city did not have to learn how to spin and weave, because cloth could be bought. However, they did learn how to tend a garden, prepare food, wash, iron, cook, bake, sew, and knit. Although they could go to the market, urban girls still learned how to preserve fruit, store vegetables, salt meat so it would not spoil, and make sausage. According to one account, Catherine Schuyler, a Dutch girl who lived in New Amsterdam, the area that is known today as New York City, grew up "perfecting herself in the arts of housekeeping. . . . The care of the dairy, the poultry, the spinning, the baking, the brewing, the immaculate cleanli-

A drawing of girls in Wethersfield, Connecticut, helping their mother weed onions.

ness of the Dutch, were not so much duties as sacred household rites."

Wealthy French Huguenot girls growing up in Charles Town, South Carolina, and wealthy girls in other colonies had private tutors who taught them dancing, music, and perhaps Greek or Latin. The girls were trained to give lavish balls and would be expected to entertain people for weeks at a time. They were also taught how to supervise the slaves who did the actual work.

Girls lived in slavery throughout the colonies. From a young age, they worked side by side with their mothers in the fields, tending to tobacco, rice, indigo, and cotton. At the beginning and end of the long days in the fields, slave girls helped their mothers prepare food and mend clothes for their families. Slave girls who lived with their masters in urban areas spent their days caring for white babies and doing household tasks. Slave girls could be sold at any time. In the early 1800s, Frances Ellen Watkins Harper witnessed such a scene and described it in a poem, "The Slave Auction:"

> The sale began—young girls were there,
> Defenceless in their wretchedness,
> Whose stifled sobs of deep despair
> Revealed their anguish and distress.
> And mothers stood with streaming eyes,
> And saw their dearest children sold.

Some black girls grew up free because their mothers had gained freedom in one of several ways—they bought their freedom with money they earned after doing their daily duties as a slave, their master or mistress freed them, or freed black men purchased them so that they could be married.

Lear Green escaped from slavery by hiding in a sailor's chest that was shipped to a free state. This drawing was made from a photograph taken shortly after she became free.

The number of free blacks increased during the seventeenth and early eighteenth centuries because the laws and attitudes regarding slavery and black people were not as oppressive and cruel as they would later become.

The experience of growing up female in Indian societies varied, although the goal was the same—to learn the role of a woman in her particular tribe. A girl's mother and the other women in her family group were the teachers. In some tribes, a girl used the same word to refer to her mother or her aunts. Their lessons were conveyed in many ways, including through songs like "A Lullaby for a Girl" from the Zuni culture.

> Little maid child!
> Little sweet one!
> Little girl!
> Though a baby,

Soon a-playing
With a baby
Will be going.
Little maid child!
Little woman so delightful!

Young Indian girls learned by playing with dolls, miniature tepees, travois (a type of carrier), and household items. According to Sharlot Hall, a historian who visited a Hopi pueblo in the northeastern corner of Arizona in which the people had preserved their ancient life and customs, "The little girls have tiny ovens and bake mud piki [a very thin bread] and play 'keep house,' and often use the younger children as their dolls and babies. They have plenty of real dolls made of carved sticks dressed in gay scraps and . . . they have very quaint dolls modeled of clay and decorated with stripes of paint and tufts of feathers."

Girls also learned by actually taking care of babies, gathering wild foods, and weeding the garden. They were taught many skills, including how to grind corn, make baskets, mats, and clothing, and do bead and embroidery work. As Sharlot Hall noted, "The women grind all the corn . . . and the girls learn to use the mealing stones at an early age. These are large flat stones on which the corn is heaped in little piles and crushed with a small stone which is turned and twisted like a rolling-pin. The piki is a very thin batter of this finely crushed corn baked on a flat rock. The bread is baked in sheets and rolled up like paper and the girl who can make it thinnest is counted the best housekeeper."

Jicarilla Apache girls who grew up in the Southwest were told from an early age to think of themselves as women able to do women's work that included knowing how to take care of horses and be good riders. Jicarilla

Indian girls with miniature tepees and dolls. The photograph was taken in Montana in the late 1800s.

girls were also expected to be strong swimmers. Girls who did not swim every day were told that lots of hair would grow between their legs, a dreaded possibility, since any body hair was considered unattractive in the Apache culture.

Indian girls also learned manners. Yurok girls who grew up in northern California were required to sit near their mothers during meals. From a young age, a girl was taught to use her spoon to take a little food from the food basket, eat slowly, and not chatter. The food basket was removed when a girl did not follow the rules, and she was expected to quietly leave the house. At the end of a meal, a girl remained seated until her father left, followed by his sons. She could leave only after her mother had cleaned out the food basket with mussel shells, rinsed them with cold water, and swept the floor over which the males had walked.

As the 1600s were coming to a close, the colonies were well established. Cities—Boston, New York, Philadelphia, Charles Town (later Charleston)—were growing. Merchants in the New England and mid-Atlantic colonies and planters in the Chesapeake and lower South colonies were accumulating great wealth. The first and second generation of white people who were born in the colonies were moving and settling in the western regions of the colonies. Mexican and Spanish settlers were expanding their settlements in the Southwest. French trappers and traders were building trading posts and forts in the midwest region. Girls were still expected to follow in their mothers' footsteps.

4

New Ideas

GIRLS IN THE LATE COLONIAL PERIOD

Eunice Williams was seven years old in 1704 when a group of French soldiers and Abenaki warriors attacked Deerfield, a frontier settlement in western Massachusetts. Most of the 268 residents were killed or taken as prisoners. Parthena, the Williams's black slave, Eunice's infant sister, and her six-year-old brother were killed. Eunice, three of her brothers, another sister, her father, and her mother were taken as prisoners. During the 300-mile march to the Abenakis' home in Canada, Eunice's mother was killed.

Two years later, the survivors of what became known as the Deerfield Massacre were ransomed. Nine-year-old Eunice, however, had been adopted by a family of Roman Catholic Iroquois who refused to return her. They said that they "would as soon part with their hearts" before they would return Eunice. In 1713 and 1714, Eunice's father visited her and asked her to return. Eunice, who had stopped speaking English, refused. In time, Eunice converted to Catholicism, married Arosen, a Catholic Iroquois, and raised a family. Years later, she visited one of her brothers, but true to the life she had chosen, Eunice remained dressed in blankets and built a wigwam, where she stayed.

In the 1740s, another girl in Deerfield left a legacy. She was Lucy Terry, a young slave in the household of Ebenezer Wells. According to

Lucy Terry by contemporary artist Louise Minks.

one account, "Lucy was a noted character and [Wells's house] a great place of resort for the young people, attracted thither by her wit and wisdom, often shown in her rhymes and stories." In 1746, when she was about sixteen years old, Lucy, who called herself Luce Bijah, wrote a poem about another Indian attack on the part of Deerfield known as "The Bars." Her poem, the earliest-known poem by a black writer in North America, included a line about how a petticoat, a multilayered garment that both girls and women wore under their skirts, hindered Eunice Allen's escape.

BARS FIGHT

August, 'twas the twenty-fifth,
Seventeen houndred forty-six,
The Indians did in ambush lay

Eunice Allen see the Indians comeing
And hoped to save herself by running;
And had not her petticoats stopt her . . .

The Deerfield Massacre and Bars Fight were two of many skirmishes and battles as English colonists moved into areas that had been long claimed by France. Native Americans, whose rights to the land were ignored by the Europeans, chose different sides. The French provided guns and offered other goods for Abenaki and Mohawk raids against English settlers. The Chickasaws and often the Cherokees, who were trading partners with the English, fought against the French. Britain was also fighting with Spain for control of Florida, a region Spain had long claimed. Finally Britain prevailed, and in 1763, a peace treaty, known as the Peace of Paris, was signed. Under the terms of the treaty, all of North America east of the Mississippi River, including Spanish Florida, became British territory.

To help pay for the war, the British had made various attempts to impose taxes or otherwise interfere in business activities of the colonies. In time, growing numbers of colonists got angry, and they protested in a variety of ways. They wrote pamphlets, songs, plays, poems, and marched in parades. Since many people could not read, meetings were held where people who could read read newspapers, articles, and pamphlets out loud.

When colonists refused to import British goods, groups of women and girls, who were often called Daughters of Liberty, gathered to make homespun cloth. "It is better to wear a Homespun coat than to lose our Liberty" was their slogan. Around their necks they wore a medallion that had a Liberty Tree, the symbol for freedom. "To the Ladies" was a very popular song that included these lyrics:

> Young ladies in town, and those that live 'round,
> Wear none but your own country linen;
> Of economy boast, let your pride be the most
> To show clothes of your own make and spinnin'.
>
> So no more ribbons wear, nor in rich silks appear,
> Love your country much better than fine things;
> Begin without passion, 'twill soon be the fashion
> To grace your smooth locks with a twine of string.
>
> What if homespun, they say, be not quite so gay
> As brocades, be not in a passion;
> For once it is known 'tis much worn in town,
> One and all will cry out, "'Tis the fashion!"

On February 21, 1772, twelve-year-old Anna Green Winslow wrote: "As I am (as we say) a daughter of liberty I chuse to wear as much of our own manufactory as pocible."

As was common in well-to-do families, Anna Green Winslow's parents had sent her to Boston in 1770 to "finish" her education. During her stay in Boston, Anna lived with an aunt and uncle and kept a journal that she sent to her parents. She wrote about going to sewing school, writing school, and learning how to dance. She noted rainy days; snowstorms; a day when "Jack Frost bites very hard, so hard aunt won't let me go to any school," and a day when "the Dust blew so that it almost put my eyes out." Anna described her clothing, including her purchase of "a very beautiful white feather hat . . . with the feathers sew'd on in a most curious manner white & unsullied as the falling snow, this hat I have long been saving my money to procure."

Occasionally Anna mentioned her ailments such as colds and sore eyes. Frequently she discussed the sermons she heard on Sunday and the lectures she attended. According to her account, Anna made "pyes"; spun linen thread and woolen yarn; knit lace; mended gloves and handkerchiefs; made shirts for her uncle and shifts for her mother; visited and dined with relatives and friends; and attended weddings, baptisms, and funerals. In one entry, Anna wrote, "I have read my bible to my aunt this morning (as is the daily custom) & sometimes I read other books to her." Anna worked hard at her writing and wrote even when she was "disabled

A page from Anna Green Winslow's journal that she sent to her parents. As was typical, she signed her full name.

by a whitloe [a boil] on my fourth finger & something like one on my middle finger."

The American Revolution began in 1775. Shortly before the war began, Jemima Condict, a young woman who lived near Morristown, New Jersey, wrote in her diary, "By What we Can hear the Quarels are not like to be made up Without bloodshed. I have jest Now heard Say that All hopes of Conciliation Between Briten & her Colonies are at an end for Both the king and his Parliament have announced our Destruction."

On April 23, Jemima wrote, "As every Day Brings New Troubels So this Day Brings News that yesterday very early in the morning They Began to fight at Boston." When the Revolution began, Anna Green Winslow was living in Marshfield, Massachusetts. Although she had identified herself as "a daughter of liberty," her father was a Loyalist, or a person who wanted to remain a citizen of England. His sister, Anna's Aunt Deming, was, too. Shortly after the Revolution began, Anna's father was exiled to England. Aunt Deming fled Boston and went to Connecticut because she could not "live in the terror of constant alarms and the din of war." Anna and her mother remained in Marshfield.

Girls and young women were actively involved throughout the war. "We may destroy all the men in America and we shall still have all we can do to defeat the women," a British officer wrote early in the war.

Betty Hager was at the scene of the first battle at Concord, Massachusetts, where the British fled and left behind six damaged cannons. Hager knew what to do with the cannons. She, and the blacksmith she worked for, fixed them to use against the British. Betty Hager had been an orphan since she was nine years old. As was the practice at that time, she was "bound out" to serve as an apprentice in the family of a machinist. Betty was so skilled at working with her hands that the machinist taught her mechanics. Betty, who was called Handy Betty, could "make almost anything out of iron or wood." She was also an expert weaver. After she had served her time as a "bound girl," Handy Betty Hager got a job with a blacksmith in Boston. She was working there at the time of the Battle of Concord. After fixing the cannons, Betty spent the rest of the war making ammunition.

As many men went off to fight, girls took over their work and responsibilities on the farms and in the cities. Some girls were camp followers, or people who followed the soldiers on the long marches and stayed in their camps. They helped cook for the soldiers, take care of the sick and wounded, mend clothes, and do laundry. Other girls helped raise money. One list of donors showed that "Polly Fritz, a little girl" gave five Continental dollars.

During the night of April 16, 1777, sixteen-year-old Sybil Ludington rode her horse forty miles to sound the alert that the British were burning Danbury, Connecticut. She roused men who belonged to her father's regiment and called them to assemble. After the battle of Danbury was won, General George Washington went to Sybil's home to thank her.

A statue of Sybil Ludington riding sidesaddle and holding the stick she used to bang on doors to awaken the sleeping militiamen.

Other young women disguised themselves as men and joined the army. Deborah Sampson became a soldier under the name Robert Shurtleff (also spelled Shirtliff or Shirtlieff). At the age of ten, Deborah had become an indentured servant. Taller and stronger than average, she plowed and planted in the fields in addition to doing her household duties. Perhaps that made it easier for Deborah to convince people that she was a man. There were rumors, however, and when the people in her church suspected what she had done, they excommunicated her for "dressing in men's clothes, and enlisting as a soldier in the Army."

A drawing of Deborah Sampson from her biography, published in 1797.

Deborah fought in several engagements. But when she was hospitalized with a fever, her sex was discovered. Although she was discharged, Deborah eventually received a pension for her military service as "a soldier of the Revolution." Deborah later married. She had two daughters, Mary and Patience.

On October 19, 1781, British Lord Cornwallis surrendered at Yorktown, Virginia. Messengers reached Philadelphia with the news three days later. Five days later, they arrived in Boston. As the news spread, celebration after celebration with parades, cannon salutes, bonfires, and fire-works took place throughout the colonies. Two years later, a formal peace treaty was signed, and the thirteen colonies became known as the United States of America.

Many new ideas were written about and discussed during the Revolution—ideas about freedom, equality, liberty, citizenship, and democracy. The emergence of these new ideas prompted some people to question the fact that growing up female during this period of history meant growing up with few, if any, educational opportunities and looking forward to very few economic or legal rights. Husbands had legal power over their wives. Typically, married women could not own property. Even their own clothes belonged to their husbands. So did any wages they earned. Married women could not sign contracts or bring lawsuits. Although divorce was rare, when it did happen a mother usually had no claim to her children.

People raised the questions in a variety of ways. "Should I not have liberty whilst you strive for liberty?" Mary Hay Barn wrote to her soldier husband. A newspaper published the following poem:

> The Equal laws let Custom find,
> And neither sex oppress;
> More freedom to Womankind
> Or give to Mankind less.

Judith Sargent Murray, who published essays under the pseudonym Constantia, wrote, "Yes, ye lordly, ye haughty sex, our souls are by nature *equal* to yours. . . . I dare confidently believe, that from the commence-ment of time to the present day, there hath been as many females, as males who by *mere force of natural powers* have merited the crown of applause." According to Judith Sargent Murray, boys were "taught to aspire" and girls were "early confined and limited. . . . The sister must be wholly domesticated, while the brother is led by the hand through all the flowery paths of science."

Eliza Wilkinson, a young woman in Charleston, South Carolina, who had maintained her parents' plantation during the war, wrote, "I won't have it thought that because we are the weaker sex as to bodily strength . . . we are capable of nothing more than minding the dairy, visiting the poultry houses, and all such domestic concerns; our thoughts can soar aloft, we

A painting of Elizabeth and Mary Daggett, who grew up in Hartford, Connecticut, in the years after the American Revolution.

can form conceptions of things of higher natures; and we have as just a sense of honor, glory, and great actions as these 'Lords of Creation.'"

In 1776, Abigail Adams wrote what is now a widely quoted letter to her husband, John, who was attending the Continental Congress and who would help write the Declaration of Independence: "In the new code of laws . . . I desire you would remember the ladies, and be more generous to them than your ancestors. Do not put such unlimited power in the hands of husbands. Remember, all men would be tyrants if they could. If particular care and attention are not paid to the ladies, we are determined to foment a rebellion, and will not hold ourselves bound to obey the laws in which we have no voice or representation."

John Adams lightly dismissed Abigail's request. He and the other men who wrote the new laws left out women's rights. This omission would affect expectations and opportunities for generations of girls.

As people continued to debate the new ideas, the new country was taking shape, and a new role emerged for many women. The role was republican motherhood, which meant being a mother who trained her sons "in the principles of liberty and government." Girls, therefore, needed to be educated in order to grow up to fulfill this new role. Benjamin Rush, a prominent physician, proposed that girls should have "a knowledge of the English language . . . a fair and legible hand [handwriting], knowledge of figures and bookkeeping . . . an acquaintance with geography . . . reading of history, travels, poetry, and moral essays." Girls should also be trained in "dancing, vocal music, . . . the Christian religion," Rush wrote.

In the years following the Revolution, many new female academies and seminaries were founded. In 1798, Judith Sargent Murray wrote, "Female academies are everywhere establishing and right pleasant is the

In 1792, Sarah Pierce began the Litchfield Female Academy in her home. This is a drawing of the building that was erected in 1798. It had "the plainest pine desks, long plank benches, a small table and an elevated teacher's chair," wrote Lucy Sheldon, a student.

appellation to my ear. . . . I may be accused of enthusiasm; but such is my confidence in THE SEX that I expect to see our young women forming a new era in female history."

The new ideas about educating girls did not apply to all girls. Certainly not to slave girls, Native American girls, or even to all white girls. One father expressed his opinion on the subject of what his daughter should learn in a poem that appeared in the *Boston Evening Post*.

> Prithee, good madam, let her first be able
> To read a chapter truly in the Bible.
>
> Make her an expert and ready at her prayer
> That God may keep her from the devil's snares;
> Teach her what's useful, how to shun deluding
> To roast, to toast, to boil and mix a pudding

To knit, to spin, to sew, to make or mend,

To scrub, to rub, to earn and not to spend,

I tell thee wife, once more, I'll have her bred

To book'ry, cookr'y, thimble, needle, thread.

Furthermore, there were no colleges for girls, even for Lucinda Foote, who at the age of twelve was tested by Ezra Stiles, president of Yale College. Stiles stated that Foote was "fully qualified" to be a pupil of the freshman class of Yale, except, Stiles added, "in regard to sex." Eventually, Lucinda Foote married and had ten children.

In the decades after the American Revolution, Vermont, Kentucky, and Tennessee had become states; Philadelphia was the largest city; slavery was on the way out in most northern states; white settlers moved westward, encroaching on Indian land every step of the way; the first

A set of kitchen toys from the 1700s.

Spanish settlers from Mexico reached Yerba Buena, now known as San Francisco; the first U.S. political parties developed; newspapers started publishing daily editions, instead of just weekly ones; the first cookbook with recipes for American specialties such as Indian pudding, pickled water-melon rind, and johnnycake was published; and girls were employed in the first water-powered textile mill.

More than four mil-lion people lived in the United States, ninety-five percent of them in rural areas. Girls were still expected to follow in their mothers' foot-steps. But growing numbers of girls, especially white girls in well-to-do families, were getting the

Eliza Southgate

education that their mothers had been denied. Eliza Southgate was one of those girls. In 1797, while she was away at school in Massachusetts, she wrote to her parents in Maine, "to think that here I may drink freely of the fountain of knowledge . . . writing, reading, and cyphering . . . French and Dancing . . . Geometry . . . Geography."

5

Making Demands

GIRLS IN THE EARLY NINETEENTH CENTURY

Lucretia Coffin's school friends called her "spitfire." She was born on January 3, 1793, and grew up during a time of transition in the history of growing up female in America. It was a time when increasing numbers of girls grew up to become women who started making demands. Lucretia Coffin was one of those girls. She was born on Nantucket Island off the coast of Massachusetts, an important sailing and whaling center. By the time she died, she had earned a place in history as Lucretia Coffin Mott, a leader in both the abolition and women's rights movements.

Lucretia's father was a sea captain who sailed back and forth to China, trading goods. Her mother ran the shop where they sold the goods. Lucretia's family belonged to the Society of

Friends, more commonly known as Quakers. The Quakers were an unpretentious people. They wore simple clothes in colors such as brown, gray, and black. Their distinct style of speech included the use of the words "thee" and "thou." Quakers believed that the "inner light" of God's guidance was in women, as well as men. Women, as well as men, could preach and teach.

As part of her education, Jane Elfreth, a Quaker girl, wrote letters to her parents. At the age of seven, she wrote this letter about going to the dentist.

Growing up Quaker on Nantucket strongly influenced Lucretia Coffin. She heard women speaking in public and preaching. Although Quaker girls were expected to grow up to be wives and mothers, they were considered equal with men in religious matters. In other matters, Quaker women were expected to defer to men. However, on Nantucket, the women typically managed every aspect of life because the men spent long periods of time at sea. "I grew up so thoroughly imbued with women's rights that it was the most important question of my life from a very early day," Lucretia later remembered.

When Lucretia was ten years old, her family moved to Boston, where she attended both private and public schools. At the age of thirteen, she went away to a Quaker boarding school. After two years, she became an assistant teacher without pay. That was when she discovered that even experienced women teachers were paid less than half of what men were paid. This was her first lesson about "the unequal condition of women." Lucretia then decided to demand for herself and other women "all that an impartial Creator had bestowed."

Lucretia Coffin Mott grew up during a time of astonishing economic and social change in America. The Industrial Revolution with its machines, mills, and factories had started slowly in the late 1700s and then exploded in the early 1800s. Many new types of jobs were created that resulted in a wider range of economic opportunities in the northeast region. These opportunities affected people differently and created new divisions in society according to wealth. Typically, these divisions are referred to as classes: lower, middle, and upper.

In the West and Southwest, the number of white settlers was growing fast. Between 1803 and 1848, the territory of the United States tripled in size as the government purchased, annexed, acquired land, removed the Indians from their lands, and fought a war with Mexico to gain more land. By 1860, there would be twenty new states, and the population would have grown from four million to more than thirty-one million.

Maryann Bacon grew up in the early 1800s.

In the South, the invention of the cotton gin in 1793 made cotton so profitable that plantation owners greatly increased the number of slaves they owned and tightened their control over them. During this time, a girl who would become a legend was growing up in slavery on a plantation in Maryland. Born Araminta, she would later be called Harriet Tubman and lead hundreds of slaves to freedom. During the Civil War, she served as a nurse, scout, and spy.

When Harriet was a young child, her master, John Brodas, hired her out to clean house and care for a baby. "I was so little that I had to sit on the floor and have the baby put in my lap," Tubman later recalled. If the baby cried or if the house was not clean enough, Harriet would be whipped. One day she ran away and hid in a pigsty for a few days. She survived by eating potato peels, until the pigs chased her away. She was returned to Brodas, who sent her to work in the fields.

Toughened by years of hard labor, Harriet grew strong. According to one account, "Before she was nineteen year old she was a match for the strongest man on the plantation. . . . She could lift huge barrels . . . and draw a loaded stone boat like an

From a young age, African-American girls took care of white girls. These girls had to stay perfectly still or the picture, called an ambrotype, would be blurry.

ox." One day while working in the field, she saw another slave slip away. The overseer went after the slave and cornered him in a store. When the overseer ordered Harriet to tie up the slave for a whipping, she refused and the slave ran out the door. The enraged overseer picked up a two-pound weight from the counter and threw it at the slave. He missed and hit Harriet instead. Her head cracked open, blood gushed out, and she collapsed in a heap. Harriet eventually recovered. For the rest of her life, however, she suffered from severe headaches and seizures that caused her to suddenly fall asleep. In the middle of conversations, while working, or even while walking, she would fall asleep. After a short time, she would wake up and go on as if nothing had happened.

During these early years of the nineteenth century, the educational opportunities for some girls, especially middle-class girls, multiplied dramatically. For the first time, some girls could go to college. The Troy Female Seminary was the first such institution to open. It was established by Emma Willard, who was born Emma Hart, the sixteenth of seventeen children, in Berlin, Connecticut.

During her girlhood, Emma was trained to follow in her mother's footsteps as a farm wife.

An 1825 painting of a domestic scene in which a girl recites the alphabet to her mother. Nearby, another girl sits with a doll on her lap and sews.

However, she also talked with her father about the new ideas for educating girls. The year she turned thirteen, Emma taught herself geometry. When she was fifteen, she went to the Berlin Academy. After a few years, Emma was placed in charge of the Berlin Academy for a term.

In time, Emma established the Troy Female Seminary, and within ten years, three hundred girls and young women were enrolled. According to one account, the students studied "reading, writing, spelling, arithmetic, grammar, geography, history, maps, and the globe, algebra, geometry, trigonometry, astronomy, natural philosophy, chemistry, botany, physiology, mineralogy, geology, and zoology in the morning; and dancing, drawing, painting, French, Italian, Spanish and German in the afternoon."

Although growing numbers of parents wanted their daughters to get a full education, the anatomy class caused consternation. "Mothers visiting a class," Emma Willard later recalled, "were so shocked at the sight of a pupil drawing a heart, arteries and veins on a blackboard to explain the circulation of blood, that they left the room in shame and dismay. To preserve the modesty of the girls, and spare them too frequent agitation, heavy paper was pasted over the pages in their textbooks which depicted the human body."

Elizabeth Cady, who as Elizabeth Cady Stanton would spearhead the drive for women's rights, attended the Troy Female Seminary. Elizabeth had grown up in Johnstown, New York. At the age of sixteen, she graduated from the Johnstown Academy, where she was the only girl in a class of boys. Although Elizabeth hoped to continue her education at Union College, where all the boys were going, she was barred because she was female. "I remember, now, how proud and handsome the boys looked in their new clothes, as they jumped into the old stage coach and drove off. . . . Again I felt more keenly than ever the humiliation of the distinctions made on the grounds of sex," she later wrote. Fortunately, however, Emma Willard's school had opened and Elizabeth was able to go there. "Mrs. Willard's Seminary at Troy was the fashionable school in my girlhood," she later recalled. "She was a splendid-looking woman . . . and fully realized my idea of a queen. . . . She gave free scholarships to a large number of promising girls, fitting them for teachers, with a proviso that, when the opportunity arose, they should, in turn, educate others."

Elizabeth's father was a lawyer in Johnstown. While she was growing up, Elizabeth spent a lot of time in her father's office "listening to the clients stating their cases, talking with the students, and reading the

Elizabeth Cady Stanton as a young woman.

laws in regard to woman." She heard many sad stories about how the law deprived married women of their earnings, their property, their children, and the ability to perform legal acts such as signing a contract.

As Elizabeth later explained, "I could not exactly understand why he could not alleviate the sufferings of these women. So, in order to enlighten me, he [her father] would take down his books and show me the inexorable statutes. The students [young male law students], observing my interest, would amuse themselves by reading to me all the worst laws they could find, over which I would laugh and cry by turns. One Christmas morning I went in to the office to show them, among other of my presents, a new coral necklace and bracelets. . . . 'Now,' said [one of the students] 'if in due time you should be my wife, these ornaments would be mine; I could take them and lock them up, and you could never wear them except with my permission. I could even exchange them for a box of cigars, and you could watch them evaporate in smoke.' "

Elizabeth resolved to take her scissors and cut every one of the "odious laws . . . out of the books; supposing my father and his library were the beginning and the end of the law." Her father heard about her plan, however, and he explained that there were many lawyers and libraries and that "if his library should burn up it would make no difference in woman's condition." Then he told Elizabeth, "When you are grown up, and able to prepare a speech you must go . . . and talk to the legislators; tell them all you have seen in this office . . . and, if you can persuade them to pass new laws, the old ones will be a dead letter."

After her graduation from the Troy Female Seminary, Elizabeth got involved in the abolition, or antislavery, movement that was gaining force in America. In 1840, she married Henry Stanton, who also was an abolitionist. After the wedding, they boarded a ship bound for London, England, to attend the World's Anti-Slavery Convention. That is where Elizabeth, the girl who planned to cut up her father's law books, met Lucretia, the girl who had been called "spitfire."

Both Henry Stanton and Lucretia Mott were delegates to the convention. However, when the convention began, they discovered that

Henry could participate, but Lucretia and the other women delegates could not. Although Henry and other men argued that the women delegates should participate, they were ignored and the women were relegated to a section behind a curtain where they could listen to the proceedings. Lucretia and Elizabeth spent much of their time in London walking "arm in arm" and talking in "a brisk fire" of words. Together they "resolved to hold a convention . . . to advocate the rights of women."

During this same period in history, advice books, conduct manuals, novels, magazines, sermons, and essays were being published to tell girls how to feel, think, and act. Because of technological advances in printing and transportation, these publications were widely available. The publications promoted the idea that girls and women and boys and men had separate spheres. The set of attitudes and expectations that had evolved for girls and women was called the "cult of true womanhood."

A girl was to grow up to be a woman whose world revolved around the home, and as a "true woman," she was expected to exhibit religious

Title page of the first Lady's Book, *which became* Godey's Lady's Book. *The editor, Sarah Josepha Hale, supported education for girls but opposed the idea of "equality with men."*

piety, sexual purity, wifely submission, and motherly domesticity. According to *Godey's Lady's Book*, the most popular women's magazine in the nineteenth century, "The perfection of womanhood . . . is the wife and mother, the center of the family, the magnet that draws man to the domestic altar, that makes him a civilized being, a social Christian. The wife is truly the light of the home."

Much of the advice for girls, especially middle-class girls, focused on what it meant to be feminine. According to the author of *How to be a Lady: A Book for Girls, Containing Useful Hints on the Formation of Character*, "Riding and driving, and even hunting and fishing are innocent amusement, as long as you undertake them in a strictly feminine spirit, and with no desire to acquire the reputation of being a *fast* girl, or a *dashing* girl, or a *jolly* girl."

Catharine E. Beecher, a teacher and widely read author, wrote, "A little girl may begin, at five or six years of age, to assist her mother; and if properly trained by the time she is ten, she can render essential aid. From this time until she is fourteen or fifteen, it should be the principal object of her education to secure a strong and healthy constitution, and a thorough practical knowledge of all kinds of domestic employments."

According to Lydia Maria Child, the author of *The Girl's Own Book*, "Every girl should know how to be useful. . . . *Every mind should seek to improve itself to the utmost*. . . . Time should be devoted *to elegant accomplishments, refined taste, and gracefulness of manner*." Child encouraged girls to play with dolls to practice sewing clothes and raising children. As Child wrote, dolls "can be scolded, and advised, and kissed, and taught to read, and sung to sleep—and anything else the fancy of the owner may devise."

Child encouraged girls to exercise, but she warned them about playing on a swing, "This game is dangerous. . . . Little girls should never be ambitious to swing higher than any of their companions." As for jump-

An illustration of girls jumping rope from The Girl's Own Book,
written in 1834 by Mrs. L. Maria Child.

ing rope, "It is healthy exercise, and tends to make the form graceful; but it should be used with moderation. I have known instances of blood vessels burst by young ladies." As for throwing snowballs, Child wrote, "I like this exercise, because it is played in the open air. Endurance of cold is a very good thing: it makes the constitution hardy. But rudeness and violence must never be allowed in this, or any other game: little girls should never forget that they are miniature ladies."

While many girls were being trained to become "miniature ladies," other girls were going to work in the growing number of textile mills. Known as mill girls, most of the girls were thirteen- to sixteen-year-old farm girls who were hired for the lowest wages: $1.45 for a six-day work week.

"When the large baggage-wagon arrived," one observer wrote, "they [farm girls] would descend from it, dressed in various and outlandish fashions, and their arms brimful of bandboxes containing all their worldly goods. . . . They had all left their pleasant country homes to try their fortunes in a great manufacturing town, and they were homesick."

Susan B. Anthony as a young woman.

Susan Brownell Anthony's father owned a cotton mill in Battenville, New York. When Susan was eleven years old, she noticed that one mill girl, Sally Ann Hyatt, knew more about weaving than did her overseer, Elijah. Susan asked her father to make Sally Ann an overseer. Her father refused because "it would never do to have a woman overseer in a mill." When Susan grew up, she worked closely with Elizabeth Cady Stanton and led the fight for women's rights.

The mill girls lived in boardinghouses that had chaperons, curfews, and strict rules, including mandatory church attendance. Their lives were regulated by bells. A bell rang to start the day at 4:30 or 5:00 in the morning and to end it at night. In between, bells rang to signal breakfast time, the start of work, lunch, back to work, and the end of work. Poems and songs were written about the bells. "Loud the morning bell is ringing" was how one poem began.

Many girls and women who worked in the mills spent their time after their long workday attending lectures, language classes, sewing groups, literary "improvement circles," and producing their own publications such as the *Lowell Offering*.

In a letter to her parents, Barilla Taylor described the details and dangers of a mill girl's life. "I like it in the mill, but my overseer is not the best, or I might say the brightest. . . . We would have a little dry bread, a cracker or two apiece and that was our dinner. . . . Ann Graham, if you know her, has got her hand tore off. It was done in the card room. I heard she has got to have it taken off above her elbow. We donts know but she will lose her life by it."

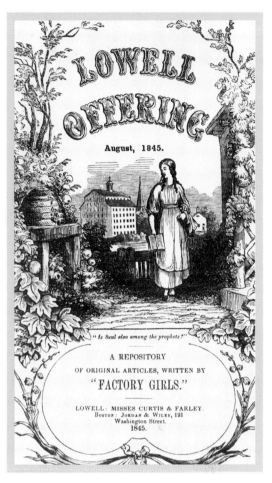

A cover from the Lowell Offering *that featured poems and stories by factory girls.*

During the 1830s, the workers became increasingly dissatisfied with the wages and working conditions. They protested by participating in "turnouts," or strikes. In 1836, eleven-year-old Harriet Hanson was one of about fifteen hundred women who protested at the mills in Lowell, Massachusetts. She later described her part in the strike: "I worked in a lower room where I had heard the proposed strike fully, if not vehemently, discussed. . . . When the day came on which the girls were to turn out, those in the upper rooms started first, and so many of them left that our mill was at once shut down. Then, when the girls in my room stood irresolute, uncertain what to do . . . I, who began to think they would not go out, after all their talk, became impatient, and started on ahead, saying, . . . 'I don't care what you do, I am going to turn out, whether anyone else does or not'; and I marched out, and was followed by the others. As I looked back at the long line that followed me, I was more proud than I have ever been."

The strikers organized the Factory Girls' Association, and they held out for one month. But then their money ran out. Girls were evicted from their boardinghouses. Although 250 skilled workers refused to return to work, others did. The strike leaders were fired. So was Harriet Hanson's mother, a widow who ran a boardinghouse. "Mrs. Hanson, you could not prevent the older girls from turning out, but your daughter is a child, and *her* you could control," a mill agent told her.

Harriet later wrote a book about her experience. According to Harriet, some of the mill workers went on to college and had businesses. One former mill girl was an artist, and another was an inventor. Some girls "were among the pioneers" in Florida and Kansas. Other girls returned to their farming villages. They were no longer "looked down upon as 'factory girls' . . . they were more often welcomed as coming from the metropolis bringing new fashions, new books, and new ideas with them." Many of them, Harriet noted, founded libraries in their hometowns.

One of Harriet's friends in the mills, Lucy Larcom, grew up to become a popular poet. According to Lucy, she wrote her first poem when she was eight years old. It was on a rainy day when she and her brother Jonathan were sitting in their favorite indoor play area, the garret. Jonathan said that they should write poems, and Lucy decided to write about the rain:

> One summer day, said little Jane,
> We were walking down a shady lane,
> When suddenly the wind blew high,
> And the red lightning flashed in the sky.
> The peals of thunder, how they rolled!
> And I felt myself a little cool'd,
> For I before had been quite warm,
> But now around me was a storm.

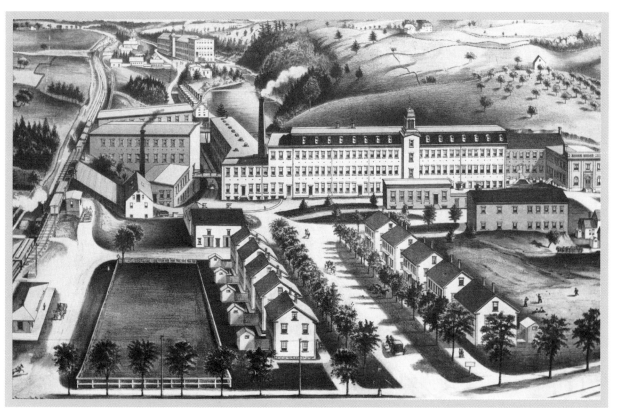

Sawyer Woolen Mills in Dover, New Hampshire, in the early 1800s.

Lucy was the ninth of ten children. She later described herself as "a homely, healthy child, having a dumpling form, round white face, gray eyes, and brown bushy hair, which was usually kept 'shingled off,' as the saying was then." Her father died when she was young, and he left behind a large debt. Lucy's mother got a job as a supervisor of a boardinghouse for mill girls in Lowell.

When Lucy was eleven years old, she went to work in the mill. Her first job was as a "doffer," which meant that she changed the bobbins on the spinning frames. It was an easy job, Lucy later wrote, although she did not like the "buzzing and hissing and whizzing of pulleys and rollers and spindles and flyers." When the "sweet June weather" came, Lucy would "lean far out of the window, and try not to hear the unceasing clash of sound inside." Next, she was a spinner and earned an average of $1.75 a week. Her sisters also worked in the mills. Lucy wrote verses and essays for one of the first mill-girl magazines that her sister Emeline started.

Lucy Larcom worked in the mills for ten years, then she did what many mill girls eventually did—she moved west.

Diverse Lives

GIRLS IN THE MID-NINETEENTH CENTURY

Lucy Larcom was one of hundreds of thousands of girls and young women who went west. For Lucy, the West in 1846 meant going from Massachusetts to Illinois. For twelve-year-old Virginia Reed, who already lived in Springfield, Illinois, going west meant going to California. Virginia left on April 15, 1846, with her mother and stepfather, grandmother, two younger brothers, and her little sister Patty. "Never can I forget the morning when we bade farewell to kindred and friends," Virginia later recalled. "We were surrounded by loved ones, and there stood all my little schoolmates who had come to kiss me good-bye. My father with tears in his eyes tried to smile as one friend after another grasped his hand in a last farewell. Mama was overcome with grief. At last we were all in the wagons,

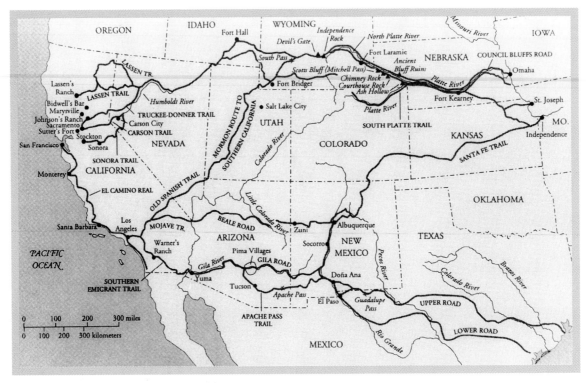

Map showing the trails to California, including the Truckee–Donner trail.

the drivers cracked their whips, the oxen moved slowly forward and the long journey had begun."

A total of thirty-one people left that day. George Donner was their leader. The Reeds left with two wagons "loaded with provisions," including "a good library." The family rode in a two-story wagon. There was a feather bed for Grandma Keyes and "spring seats with comfortable high backs" and a "tiny sheet-iron stove, whose pipe, running through the top of the wagon, was prevented by a circle of tin from setting fire to the canvas cover." The "large and roomy second story" had beds for the rest of the family. Their clothes were packed "in strong canvas bags plainly marked." Directly opposite the door, Virginia later wrote, "Some of mama's young friends added a looking-glass . . . in order, as they said, that my mother might not forget to keep her good looks." The Reeds had oxen, saddle horses, cows, and Virginia's pony Billy. "He was a beauty," Virginia recalled.

According to Virginia, the trip was uneventful until they reached what is now known as Kansas. She had grown up listening to her grandmother tell stories about how Indians in Kentucky had taken an aunt prisoner and held her captive for five years. In Kansas, Virginia reported, "The first Indians we met were the Caws, who kept the ferry, and had to take us over the Caw River. I watched them closely, hardly daring to draw my breath, and feeling sure they would sink the boat in the middle of the stream, and was very thankful when I found they were not like grandma's Indians."

A wagon train headed west.

Virginia's grandma died in Kansas on May 29. "It seemed hard to bury her in the wilderness, and travel on . . . but her death here, before our troubles began, was providential, and nowhere on the whole road could we have found so beautiful a resting place. . . . A coffin was hewed out of a cottonwood tree, and John Denton . . . found a large gray stone on which he carved with deep letters the name of 'Sarah Keyes; born in Virginia,' giving age and date of birth. She was buried under the shade of an oak, the slab being placed at the foot of the grave, on which were planted wild flowers growing in the sod," Virginia later recalled.

The group continued their journey. Along the way, other people in wagons joined them. Virginia spent her days riding Billy: "How I enjoyed riding my pony, galloping over the plain, gathering wild flowers!" In July, they reached Wyoming, where, Virginia later wrote, "A day came when I had no pony to ride, the poor little fellow gave out. He could not endure the hardships of ceaseless travel. When I was forced to part with him I cried until I was ill, and sat in the back of the wagon watching him become smaller and smaller as we drove on, until I could see him no more."

In September, they crossed the desert in Utah, where there was relentless heat and few sources of water. The Reeds' oxen "began to fall to the ground from thirst and exhaustion." Finally, they had to abandon their two-story family wagon and one of the provision wagons. In October, the group reached Nevada, where Virginia's stepfather got in a fight with a man who was "beating his cattle over the head with the butt end of his whip." During the fight, the man was killed. "The members of the Donner party," Virginia wrote later, "refused to accept the plea of self-defense and decided that my father should be banished from the company and sent into the wilderness alone. . . . I followed him through the darkness . . . and carried him his rifle, pistols, ammunition and some food. . . . I had

An artist's depiction of the Donner party struggling through the snow.

cried until I had hardly strength to walk [back to camp], but when . . . I saw the distress of my mother, with the little ones clinging around her, . . . it seemed suddenly to make a woman of me."

In the last week of October, Virginia later reported, the party reached California and tried to cross the Sierra Nevada Mountains. However, "Winter had set in a month earlier than usual. . . . Despair drove many nearly frantic. That night came the dreaded snow. Around the campfires under the trees great feathery flakes came whirling down. The air was so full of them that one could see objects only a few feet away. . . . We children slept soundly on our cold bed of snow with a soft white mantle falling over us so thickly that every few moments my mother would have to shake the shawl—our only covering to keep us from being buried alive."

The group took refuge in three cabins that they found at a lake that would later be called Donner Lake. Fifteen people—ten men and five women—made snowshoes and set out to get help. Seven of them—two of the men and all five women—eventually reached San Francisco. In February, the first rescue party arrived. Of the eighty-three people who were snowed in, forty-two had died. With her mother, brothers, and sister, Virginia had survived. They had eaten twigs, mice, their shoes, and animals' hides that covered the roof of their cabin. Some of the other survivors had resorted to cannibalism and eaten their own dead.

Virginia and her family left with the first relief party. On the way, they met her father, who had come back in search of them. Surviving freezing weather and fierce snowstorms, they finally reached safety. "Patty [her younger sister] was not alone in her travels," Virginia later wrote. "Hidden away in her bosom was a tiny doll, which she had carried day and night through all our trials."

Patty Reed's doll.

Thocmetony, or Shell Flower, was very young when she first heard members of her tribe talk about how the members of the Donner party survived by resorting to cannibalism. Shell Flower, later known as Sarah Winnemucca, was born about 1844 among the Paiute tribe who lived in the high desert country at the Humboldt Sink in what is now Nevada. Her grandfather trusted white people and he guided groups of white explorers. Her father and mother, however, were very wary. They knew about the Donner party. They also knew that white people killed Indians and destroyed their food supply.

Once, when her mother and aunt were gathering seeds and roots with Shell Flower and her cousin Elma, they saw white people coming. To keep the girls safe, Shell Flower's mother and aunt decided to bury the girls. According to Shell Flower, "Our mothers buried me and my cousin, planted sage bushes over our faces to keep the sun from burning them, and there we were left all day. . . . Oh, can any one imagine my feelings *buried alive*, thinking every minute that I was to be unburied and eaten up by the people that my grandfather loved so much? . . . At last we heard some whispering. . . . I could hear their footsteps coming nearer and nearer. I thought my heart was coming right out of my mouth. Then I heard my mother say, 'Tis right here!' Oh, can any one in this world ever imagine what were my feelings when I was dug up."

Sarah Winnemucca became a passionate crusader for the rights of her people. She spoke five languages and was an interpreter and teacher. Her book, *Life Among the Piutes* (another spelling of the tribe's name), was the first book about Indians by an Indian woman. She spoke to white audiences and government officials, including a president of the United States. "The proverb says the big fish eat up the little fishes and we Indians are the little

Sarah Winnemucca

fish and you eat us all up and drive us from home," she told her audiences. Winnemucca's pleas did not stop the settlers. They kept coming, especially after the discovery of gold in California in 1848.

That was the same year Elizabeth Cady Stanton and Lucretia Mott got together again at the home of a friend in upstate New York. Eight years had passed since they met at the World's Anti-Slavery Convention in London, England. During that time, Mott was deeply involved in the fight to end slavery. Stanton was immersed in the responsibilities of being the mother of three young children. Now, however, as they drank tea and discussed the status of women with three other women, they decided the time had come to hold a convention to "advocate the rights of women." Stanton took charge and put a notice in the local newspaper saying that the convention would be held in Seneca Falls, New York, on July 19 and 20.

Although it was the middle of haying season, more than three hundred people came. They walked and rode in wagons and buggies. The centerpiece of the convention was the Declaration of Sentiments that Elizabeth Cady Stanton wrote. The Declaration of Sentiments stated that "all men and women are created equal" and highlighted the lack of education and economic opportunities for women. Sixty-eight women and thirty-two men signed the Declaration of Sentiments. Although this convention was denounced and ridiculed, it launched a struggle for rights and opportunities that would eventually transform the world for future generations of girls growing up in America.

Three years after the convention, a furor erupted over a fashion innovation designed to free females from the constraints of petticoats and skirts that dragged on the ground. The fuss was over bloomers, baggy pants worn under a short skirt. Some girls had worn straight-leg pants, known as pantalettes or pantaloons, under their frock since the 1820s. But not without criticism. When Sara Hutchinson heard in 1824 that her niece was wearing pants under her frock, she wrote, "I am sorry to hear that dear little Good-Good has been breeched. . . . It is much better that females should not." In 1849, ten-year-old Catherine Havens wrote in her diary about a schoolmate whose step-mother made her wear beige pantalettes: "The boys tease her and call her ginger legs and she is very unhappy. It is a very sad case."

In 1851, the idea of bloomers made the critics go crazy. The new style was named for Amelia Bloomer, who lived in Seneca Falls and had attended the first Women's Rights Convention. Bloomer championed the new style in her newspaper, *The Lily*. She pointed out how the tight, stiff corsets and long, heavy skirts that were the fashion of the time hindered women and damaged their health. From an early age, many girls wore corsets. By the time a girl was seven or eight, her mother might peri-odically tighten the corset so that she would develop a very skinny waist, known as "wasp waist."

Bloomer received a flood of letters from women requesting pat-terns to make bloomers, and many new subscribers to her newspaper.

An 1851 illustration of a young woman wearing bloomers.

But the public ridicule directed at women who wore bloomers proved to be too much. According to Elizabeth Cady Stanton, "People would stare, many men and women would make rude remarks, boys followed in crowds with jeers and laughter." Within two years, most women had stopped wearing bloomers, including Elizabeth Cady Stanton.

By the mid-nineteenth century, Americans were deeply divided over the issue of slavery. The abolition movement had been growing since the beginning of the century. In 1852, Harriet Beecher Stowe, who was an abolitionist, wrote *Uncle Tom's Cabin*. The best-selling book relates the story of Tom, a slave who saves the life of Eva St. Clair, a wealthy white girl. Eva persuades her father to buy Tom. Countless numbers of girls read an abridged version that was published for children.

Despite strong taboos against women speaking in public, many women spoke out against slavery. Hostile crowds booed, jeered, threw rotten food and rocks, and set fires, but the women continued to speak out. Louise Thomas later recalled, "When I was a little girl scarcely nine years old, my mother said to me, 'Some day the slaves will be free, dear'—and I remember to this day how her prophecy puzzled me—how I could not comprehend how that possibly could ever be."

Paper dolls of Topsey (above) and Eva St. Claire (left), two characters from Uncle Tom's Cabin *by Harriet Beecher Stowe.*

Louise grew up forty miles west of Union Springs, New York, directly on one of the routes of what was called the Underground Railroad, a network of thousands of white and free black people who helped runaway slaves get to freedom in northern states and Canada. Louise's neighbors, the Smiths, frequently concealed runaway slaves. According to Louise, "The whole matter of rescuing the slaves had to be carried on with great care, even among some of the Northern people. There was one occasion when our neighbor had some slaves concealed in the attic. . . . The slaves, of course, had to be fed and it was Mrs. Smith's habit to take the food up to them. This day there were visitors in the house whom our neighbor did not quite trust. It was also time to feed the fugitives upstairs. So Mrs. Smith secured a clothesbasket, put the food in the bottom and then after telling the folks that her wash just had to be taken upstairs she took the negroes their food."

Girls growing up during the mid-nineteenth century were living increasingly diverse lives. Anna Howard Shaw immigrated to America from England when she was four years old. She lived first in the seaport town of New Bedford, Massachusetts, where her best friend was a ship-builder who lived next door. "Morning after morning this man swung me on his big shoulder and took me to his shipyard, where my hatchet and saw [toy ones her father had given her] had violent exercise as I imitated the workers around me. Discovering that my tiny petticoats were in my way, my new friend had a little boy's suit made for me; and thus emancipated me at this tender age," she later wrote.

Next, Anna lived in Lawrence, Massachusetts, a thriving factory town, where she learned about the Underground Railroad. As she later recalled, "One day, in visiting our cellar, I heard a noise in the coal-bin. I investigated and discovered a negro woman concealed there. I had been reading *Uncle Tom's Cabin*, as well as listening to the conversations of my elders, so I was vastly stirred over the negro question. I raced upstairs in a condition of awe-struck and quivering excitement, which my mother promptly suppressed by sending me to bed. No doubt she questioned my youthful discretion, for she almost convinced me that I had seen nothing at all—almost, but not quite; and she wisely kept me close to her for several days, until the escaped slave . . . was safely out of the house and away."

Two sisters who grew up during the mid-nineteenth century.

Anna also remembered spending her first twenty-five cents while she lived in Lawrence. "I used an entire day in doing this. . . . The first place we [Anna and her sister Mary] visited was a candy store. . . . We forced the weary proprietor to take down and show us every jar in the place before we spent one penny. The first banana I ever ate was purchased that day, and I hesitated over it a long time. Its cost was five cents, and in view of that large expenditure, the eating of the fruit, I was afraid, would be too brief a joy. I bought it, however, not knowing enough to peel the banana, I bit through the skin and pulp alike, as if I were eat-

A girl stands by the sod wall of her family's dugout house in Nebraska. Her brother sits on a swing.
The woman in the suit was perhaps a teacher who boarded with them.
The wagon on the roof contains a load of sod blocks, perhaps to add a room.

ing an apple, and then burst into tears of disappointment."

When Anna was twelve years old, she, her two older sisters, little brother, and mother moved to the Michigan frontier. Her father had gone ahead and built a cabin nine miles from the nearest settlement. She later described her mother's reaction when they arrived at the crude cabin with dirt floors and square holes for the door and windows: "It was late in the afternoon. . . . My mother . . . crossed the threshold and, standing very still, looked slowly around her. Then something within her seemed to give way, and she sank upon the floor. She could not realize even then, I think, that this was really the place father had prepared for us, that here he expected us to live. When she finally took it in she buried her face in her hands, and in that way she sat for hours, without speaking or moving."

When her father and older brothers left for eighteen months to earn money, Anna and her siblings took over because her mother never fully overcame her despair. Her sisters took over the domestic duties. Anna, who was twelve years old, and Henry, who was eight years old, cut wood, hauled water, gathered wild fruit, and made furniture. Anna later described how they grew food: "We took an ax, chopped up the sod, put the seed under it, and let the seed grow. . . . Our green corn and potatoes were the best I have ever eaten." She and Henry also fished in a nearby stream: "We had no hook or lines, but he took wires from our hoop-skirts and made snares at the ends of poles. My part of this work was to stand on a log and frighten fish out of their holes by making horrible sounds. . . . When the fish hurried to the surface . . . to investigate the appalling noises . . . they were easily snared."

Anna's father did return in eighteen months and he "brought with him a rocking-chair for mother and a new supply of books, on which I fell as a starving man falls upon food."

By the time Anna was fifteen, there were enough settlers that she became a schoolteacher for two dollars a week and board. "I 'boarded round' with the families of my pupils, staying two weeks in each place, and often walking from three to six miles a day to and from my little log schoolhouse in every kind of weather," Anna later explained. "During the first year I had about fourteen pupils, of varying ages, sizes, and temperaments, and there was hardly a book in the schoolroom except those I owned. One little girl, I remember, read from an almanac, while a second used a hymnbook. . . . In 'boarding round' I often found myself in one-room cabins, with bunks at the end and the sole partition a sheet or a blanket, behind which I slept with one or two of the children. It was the custom on these occasions for the man of the house to delicately retire to the barn while we women got to bed, and to disappear again in the morning while we dressed. In some places the meals were so badly cooked that I could not eat them, and often the only food my poor little pupils brought to school for their noonday meal was a piece of bread or a bit of raw pork."

While Anna Howard Shaw was growing up female in Massachusetts and Michigan, other girls were living very different lives. Maria Ascension Sepulveda was growing up on Rancho San Joaquin near Los Angeles, California. When she was nine years old, her parents sent her to the Convent of Notre Dame in San Jose where she learned English, French, sewing, and music. Maria later described a visit by her father in 1856: "He took me riding around San Jose where we visited a French rose nursery. That was the first time I had ever seen cultivated roses, and I was so enthusiastic that I made my father buy a wagon load of blooms for the Sisters."

Margarita Enriquez was growing up in San Miguel, New Mexico. Her mother, Doña Inez Ramírez, was part

Daughters and granddaughters of Mariano Guadalope Vallejo, a wealthy ranchero in California. He and his wife, Benicia, had sixteen children, and each child had a servant.

A drawing of girls taking a train trip. In the 1860s, trains went only part of the way to the West. In 1869, when the transcontinental railroad was completed, a trip to San Francisco took four days; by wagon it took about four months. But settlers traveling by wagon could go to remote places and bring more of their possessions.

Apache, and her father was one of the earliest settlers from Mexico. The big living room in Margarita's house was the center of the social life in the village. People gathered there for dances, baptisms, and other events because their small adobe church did not have a hall.

Recent immigrant girls from Ireland, who oftentimes came alone and were typically nicknamed Bridget by employers, were growing up in crowded cities such as Boston and New York, and working as domestic servants. Other girls who were immigrating with their families from Germany, Norway, Sweden, and Finland were growing up on the frontier in the West and Midwest, including Minnesota, Nebraska, and Oregon. In the mid-nineteenth century, white females on the frontier, both native born and immigrant, were still scarce, so girls as young as ten years old were courted by men looking for wives. It was not uncommon for a girl to marry at age thirteen or fourteen. Financially successful men would take out newspaper advertisements. One such notice read: "Wanted a WIFE, from 14 to 25 years of age. She must be . . . inclined to industry . . . capable of arranging a dinner table in the most modern style, also of entering a drawing or ball room gracefully . . . and partial to children."

Eleven-year-old Martha Gentry was growing up as her parents moved from one gold mining camp to another in northern California. "One day a miner gave me and the other children permission to dig on his claim. . . . Diligently we set out to work, and carefully scooped up the soft dirt and then washed it, just as we had seen the men do many times. I was the luckiest one in the group, and found a nugget worth five dollars. With this I bought a pair of shoes, of which I was sorely in need."

Chona, a Papago Indian (now called Tohono O'Odham), was growing up in the Southwest. As an old woman, she recalled, "We lived in Mesquite Root and my father was chief there. That was a good place, high up among the hills, but flat, with a little wash where you could plant corn. Prickly pear grew there so thick in summer, when you picked fruit, it was only four steps from one bush to the next. And cholla cactus grew and there were ironwood trees. Good nuts they have! There were birds flying around, doves and woodpeckers, and a big rabbit sometimes in the early morning, and quails running across the flat land. Right above us was Quijotoa Mountain, the one where the cloud stands up high and white when we sing for rain.

We lived in a grass house. . . . All our family slept on cactus fiber mats against the wall, pushed tight against it so centipedes and scorpions could not crawl in. There was a mat for each two children, but no, nothing over us. When we were cold, we put wood on the fire."

Josephine Smith was growing up female as a slave in Norfolk, Virginia. "I remembers the day we was put on the block at Richmond," she recalled. "I was just toddling around then, but me and my mammy brought a thousand dollars. My daddy, I reckon, belonged to somebody else, and we was just sold away from him. . . . I ain't had much clothes, and I ain't had so much to eat, and a-many a whupping."

Harriet Ann Jacobs spent seven years of her girlhood hiding in the crawl space of an attic to avoid the sexual aggressions of her slaveowner. "Countless were the nights that I sat late at the little loophole scarcely large enough to give me a glimpse of one twinkling star," she later wrote. "There, I heard the patrols and slave-hunters conferring together about

Girls and women picking cotton.

the capture of runaways, well knowing how rejoiced they would be to catch me." After she finally escaped, Jacobs wrote a widely read book, *Incidents in the Life of a Slave Girl: Written by Herself.*

Elleanore Eldridge, a free black girl, was growing up with a white family in Warwick, Rhode Island. When Elleanore was ten, her mother died. The white family her mother worked for invited Elleanore to live with them. Elleanore, who had been named after the white woman, agreed. According to one account, Elleanore learned "every kind of spinning; and plain, double and ornamental weaving. . . . There are few girls . . . capable of mastering such an intricate business."

Carolyn Cowles Richards was growing up female in a small village. Her mother had died when she was seven years old. As was common at the time, her father sent her and her sister Anna and brothers John and James to live with their grandparents in Canandaigua, New York. On her tenth birthday, November 21, 1852, Carolyn started her diary. Anna was seven years old. John and James were away at boarding school. Carolyn wrote about school; buggy rides with her grandfather; conversations with her grandmother; sewing doll clothes with Anna; playing snap the whip, "mumble te peg," and "Cat's Cradle;" and rolling her hoop in the garden.

On a day that her father and uncle visited, she wrote about going to a store: "[They] told us we could have anything we wanted. So we asked for several kinds of candy, stick candy and lemon drops and bulls' eyes, and then they got us two rubber balls and two jumping ropes with handles and two hoops and sticks to roll them with and two red carnelian rings and two bracelets."

On December 20, 1855, Carolyn, who was then thirteen years old, wrote about going to see Susan B. Anthony, a leader in the fight for women's rights: "Susan B. Anthony is in town and spoke in Bemis Hall this afternoon. She made a special request that all the seminary girls should come to hear her as well as all the women and girls in town. She had a large audience and she talked very plainly about our rights and how we ought to stand up for them, and said the world would never go right until the women had just as much right to vote and rule as the men. She asked us all to come up and sign our names who would promise to do all in our power to bring about that glad day when equal rights should be the law of the land. A whole lot of us went up and signed the paper. When I told Grandmother about it she said she guessed Susan B. Anthony had forgotten that St. Paul said the women should keep silence. I told her, no, she didn't, for she spoke particularly about St. Paul and said if he had lived in these times, instead of 1800 years ago, he would have been as anxious to have the women at the head of the government as she was. I could not make Grandmother agree with her at all and she said we might better all of us stayed home."

Carolyn Richards

In 1859, Carolyn and her friends formed the Young Ladies Sewing Society. The purpose was to have "great fun and fine suppers," and make each member a "quilt with all our names on when they are married. Susie Daggett says she is never going to be married, but we must make her a quilt just the same."

In the spring of 1861, Carolyn wrote the following entries:

March 4, 1861. President Lincoln was inaugurated today.

March 5. I read the inaugural address aloud to Grandfather this evening. He dwelt with such pathos upon the duty that all, both North and South, owe to the Union, it does not seem as though there could be war!

April. We seem to have come to a sad, sad time. . . . Men are taking sides, some for the North, some for the South. Hot words and fierce looks have followed, and there has been a storm in the air for a long time.

The quilt Carolyn Richards and her friends made for Mary Field. Each girl signed the quilt and wrote verses and quotations, including some by Shakespeare and many from the Bible.

April 15. The storm has broken upon us. The Confederates fired on Fort Sumter, just off the coast of South Carolina, and forced her on April 14 to haul down the flag and surrender. President Lincoln issued a call for 75,000 men and many are volunteering to go all around us. How strange and awful it seems.

May, 1861. Many of the young men are going. . . . It seems very patriotic and grand when they are singing 'It is sweet, Oh, 'tis sweet, for one's country to die,' and we hear the martial music and see the flags flying. . . but it will not seem so grand if we hear they are dead on the battlefields, far from home.

The news of war spread rapidly. According to Anna Howard Shaw, "When the news came that Fort Sumter had been fired on, and that Lincoln had called for troops, our men were threshing. . . . I remember seeing a man ride up on horseback, shouting out Lincoln's demand for troops and explaining that a regiment was being formed at Big Rapids [Michigan]. Before he had finished speaking, the men on the machine had leaped to the ground and rushed off to enlist. . . . In ten minutes not a man was left in the field."

Hannah Crasson, a slave who was about twelve years old, later talked about the reaction on Walton's plantation in Raleigh, North Carolina: "I remember the day the war commenced. My marster called my father and my two uncles, Handy and Hyman. . . . He told them, 'There is a war commenced between the North and the South. If the North whups, you will be as free a man as I is. If the South whups, you will be a slave all your days.'

"Mr. Joe Walton said when he went to war that they could eat breakfast at home, go and whup the North, and be back for dinner. He went away, and it was four long years before he come back to dinner. The table was sure set a long time for him. A lot of white folks said there wouldn't be much war, they could whup them so easy. Many of them never did come back to dinner."

The Civil War lasted four full years and involved more than 2,200 battles. The war spread from South Carolina to Virginia, Minnesota, Florida, New Mexico, and Oregon; cost more than eight billion dollars; and resulted in almost a half-million casualties. When the men left to fight, girls and women took over. They ran the farms so well that the annual production of wheat and wool increased every year of the war. In June of 1863, there was an article in the

Rose Greenhow, known as Little Rose, and her mother, Rose. A spy for the Confederacy, Rose was arrested and put in Old Capitol Prison. Little Rose went, too. This picture was taken in the prison.

Decatur, Illinois, *Magnet* about a "young woman about 19 years old . . . who takes the lead at agricultural labor. One of her brothers is in the army, one . . . sent home a cripple, and the father is also disabled, so she has gone into the fields and about three weeks ago covered 1,050 hills of corn in five hours." A popular song at the time had these lyrics:

> Just take your gun and go;
> For Ruth can drive the oxen, John,
> And I can use the hoe.

There were many other ways that girls and women participated during the war. They went to work in newly opened factories that made a variety of goods, including munitions and uniforms. They held ice-cream-and-cake socials and huge fairs that raised from $25 to over $350,000. They stitched shirts, knit socks, made bandages, and scraped lint that was used to pack wounds. Elizabeth Cady Stanton's daughter Harriot later recalled, "It is as clear as if it were yesterday's experience, sitting in the dining room of our house . . . scraping lint for the wounded in the hospital. My mother and Maggie [her sister] . . . cutting the old linen into small squares which . . . I then unravelled into lint."

Carolyn Richards recorded some of what she and her friends did a month after the war began in May, 1861: "A lot of us girls went down to the train and took flowers to the soldiers as they were passing through and they cut buttons from their coats and gave them to us as souvenirs. We have flags on our paper and envelopes, and have all our stationery bordered with red, white and blue. We wear little flag pins for badges and have pins and earrings made of the buttons the soldiers gave us. We are going to sew for them in our society. . . . We are going to write notes and enclose them in the garments to cheer up the soldier boy."

Other girls and women were scouts, spies, and soldiers in both the Union and Confederate armies. Today in Gadsden, Alabama, there is a large statue of Emma Sansom. At the age of fifteen, she guided a Confederate general to a shortcut that enabled him to capture many Union soldiers. Jennie Hodges of Illinois disguised herself as Albert Cashier and fought for four years. Hodges received a pension as a male soldier until 1911, when an automobile accident forced "him" to get medical treatment. Elizabeth Van Lew, a middle-aged white woman, and Mary Elizabeth Bowser, a young black woman, worked closely together as Union spies in Richmond, Virginia, the capital of the Confederacy. Susie Baker King Taylor escaped from slavery during the war when she was thirteen years old. Susie knew how to read because two white children and a free black woman had secretly taught her while she was a slave. Once free, Susie taught reading to other slaves who had escaped. She also served as a nurse for the Union soldiers.

As the war continued, many girls and women endured suffering and hardship. Battles were fought in and around the towns and cities where they lived. Fathers, uncles, and

Nellie Grant, the daughter of General Ulysess S. Grant, raised money for the war effort at a fair by portraying "the old woman who lived in a shoe" and selling dolls.

brothers were wounded, disabled, and killed. In the South, where many battles were fought, civilians were scrounging to find food, shoes, clothing, and other supplies. In 1864, Carrie Berry, who was ten years old and lived in Atlanta, Georgia, wrote in her diary that she hoped that by the time she turned eleven "we will have peace in our land and I can have a nice dinner."

Peace finally came on April 9, 1865, when General Robert E. Lee surrendered. "Lee has surrendered! . . . Boys and girls, men and women are running through the streets wild with excitement. . . . I am going down town again now, with my flag in one hand and bell in the other and make all the noise I can," wrote Carolyn Richards. Mary Anderson, who was fourteen years old and a slave, remembered that the "Marster and Missus come out on the porch and stood side by side. You could hear a pin drop. . . . They were both crying. Then Marster said, 'Men, women, and children, you are free. You are no longer my slaves.'"

*Former slaves, including three girls, who were photographed
on Saint Helena Island, South Carolina,
shortly after the end of the Civil War.*

7

New Opportunities

GIRLS IN THE LATE NINETEENTH CENTURY

María Concepción Garza and her sister, María del Carmen Garza, were born in south Texas near the end of the nineteenth century. They were Tejanas, descendants of the Spanish and Mexican settlers in the Lower Rio Grande Valley. According to the sisters, "*ranchero* families and friends were very united." Another Tejana, Emilia Schunior Ramirez, said, "Everyone knew everyone else, and though the means of communication and transportation were scarce, there was a feeling of kinship. . . among all the early settlers." Family life in south Texas included traditional family feasts; *quinceañera* celebrations for a girl's fifteenth birthday; the playing of music in the main plaza; and *funciones* (public dances) that were held at someone's *rancho*.

At the celebrations, musicians performed and poets wrote

corridos (ballads) in honor of a special person or event. Religious holidays were celebrated, such as the Day of the Three Wise Kings on January 6. That was the day family members exchanged gifts. During times of *secas* (drought), everyone prayed to Saint Isidore, the patron saint of farmers. According to the Garza sisters, the "people would gather, lead a procession along paths around the fields until a spot was found and San Isidro was placed on a niche. When the rains finally came, the rosary was prayed in thanksgiving for nine days."

The late nineteenth century was a time of enormous change in America. Virtually every aspect of life speeded up. Industrialization accelerated and new industries and big businesses appeared, including steel plants, oil refineries, and railroad companies. Cities grew rapidly as people abandoned farm life to work and live in urban areas. The nation's wealth continued to increase dramatically and unevenly. Women had gained full suffrage, or the right to vote, in two territories—Wyoming and Utah, although not in any of the states. After being fashionable for most of

A picture of a Mexican girl that was taken about 1890 in the Southwest.

the 1800s, hoopskirts finally went out of style. Over the years the hoops had become so wide that a single dress required at least twenty-five yards of material. Some young women wore hip and back pads to support the heavy weight of so much fashion. Hoopskirts were replaced by bustles that elevated just the back part of the skirt.

Many girls, especially white middle- and upper-class girls, were still being trained in the ways of "true womanhood." Instructions and advice came from songs, sermons, stories, novels, magazines, and etiquette

Four "little ladies" who grew up during the late 1800s having an Easter party with eggs and live chickens.

books. Girls were told how to walk, talk, laugh, pray, play with dolls, stand, sit, smile, hold a fan, obey, and faint. A list of rules published in *Good Housekeeping* magazine advised parents to teach the following table manners: "Teach it [the child] to take its seat quietly; To use its napkin properly; To wait patiently to be served; . . . Never to interrupt and never to contradict; Never to make remarks about the food; . . . To always say 'Excuse me, please,' to the mother when at home or to the lady or hostess when visiting, if leaving the table before the rest of the party. . . ."

Lina Beard and her sister Adelia B. Beard wrote *The American Girls Handy Book* in order to provide "healthy sensible work and amusement for leisure hours . . . to refine the tastes and ambitions of our American girls." Their chapter titles include "The Walking Club," "Sea-Side Cottage Decoration," "How to Make a Fan," "Window Decorations," and "Home-Made Candy."

Some girls, however, had their own ideas, including Martha "Minnie" Carey Thomas, who would grow up to be a college president and fiery speaker for suffrage. The year she was fourteen years old, Minnie attended a lecture in Baltimore on women's rights by Anna Dickinson. After hearing her, Minnie wrote in her diary:

January 6 [1871]. After supper we went to Anna Dickinson's lecture. . . . A girl certainly [should] do what she chooses as well as a boy. When I grow up—we'll see what happens.

Dr. Morris walked home with us and talked all the while about the 'sacred shrine of womanhood' and no matter what splendid talents a woman might have she couldn't use them better than by being a wife and mother. . . . Bah! Stuff and nonsense!

On October 1, 1871, Minnie wrote:

Oh I think it's cruel when a girl wants to go to college and learn and she can't and is laughed at and absolutely kept from it while a *boy* is made to go whether he wants to or not. I don't see why the world is made so unjust and I don't see why all unjustness should be turned against girls in general and me in particular. More and more every day I'm making up my mind to be a doctor for when I grow up I can't be dependent on father and mother and I ain't going to get married. . . . I can't imagine anything worse than living a regular young ladies life. . . . I *despise* society.

During the late 1800s, girls were reading books that had been written specifically for them, including the enormously popular *Little Women* by Louisa May Alcott. She had been asked to write the book by a publisher who thought that books written just for girls might sell. Alcott agreed to write such a book, although she had a full-time job as an editor for a girls' magazine called *Merry Museum*.

Drawing on experiences from her own girlhood, Alcott wrote about the lives of four sisters in the March family—the high-spirited Jo, kind Meg, sensitive Beth, and the sometimes infuriating Amy. Alcott modeled Jo after herself. In a diary that

Little Miss Giant was a popular girls' book that began: "There was a saucy giant girl/Of most amazing size."

Alcott kept when she was a girl, she wrote, "I always thought I must have been a deer or a horse in a former state, because it was such a joy to run. No boy could be my friend till I had beaten him in a race, and no girl if she refused to climb trees, leap fences, and be a tomboy."

Louisa May Alcott never married. Neither did Sarah Orne Jewett, who published her first story in 1863 when she was fourteen years old, and grew up to become a well-known author. Girls who read Jewett's books encountered a number of independent and feisty young girls who were free to run in the woods and get dirty, including Nan Prince in *A Country Doctor* and Sylvie in *A White Heron*. In Jewett's best-known book, *The Country of the Pointed Firs,* she created Joanna, who lived for twenty years on a remote island.

Sarah Orne Jewett

By the 1870s and 1880s, women like Louisa May Alcott and Sarah Orne Jewett were being labeled as New Women—independent, well-educated, professional women who were usually single.

A variety of factors made life as a New Woman possible. Laws that restricted women's legal rights were slowly being changed. The number of schools and colleges for girls and women continued to increase dramatically. New industries and businesses were creating more job opportunities. The experience many girls and women gained during the Civil War brought about changes, too. "American women no longer followed in the dull beaten track of example, but striking out into new and untried paths. . . . War enabled her to rise to a measure of usefulness that was hitherto even by herself undreamed of," explained Stella Coatsworth, who served as a nurse during the Civil War.

Another factor was the growing visibility of the first generation of women who had managed to overcome barriers to enter previously all-male professions. These women provided new role models for girls. One such woman was Maria Mitchell, who studied the skies when she was a young girl and grew up to become a famous astronomer and a professor at Vassar College. When the rules that regulated feminine behavior interfered with education, Mitchell did not hesitate to ignore them. In particular, she ignored the night curfew that would have prevented her students from studying the stars.

Anna Howard Shaw later recalled what it meant for her to meet a woman minister. "It was a wonderful moment when I saw my first woman minister enter her pulpit; and as I listened to her sermon, thrilled to the soul, all my early aspirations to become a minister myself stirred in me. . . . After the service I hung for a time on the fringe of the group that surrounded her, and, at last, when she was alone and about to leave, I found courage to introduce myself and pour forth the tale of my ambition. Her advice was prompt. . . . 'My child,' she said, 'You can't do anything until you have an education. Get it, and get it *now*.'"

Frances Willard was another important model during this period. She was active in the suffrage movement as well as the leader of the temperance movement, the fight against alcohol abuse. When Frances was a girl in the

Wisconsin Territory, she had worn her hair short and insisted on being called "Frank." On her sixteenth birthday, however, her mother said that Frances could no longer run "wild." Instead she had to put on the "hampering long skirts . . . with their accompanying corset and high heels." From that time until she was fifty-three years old, Frances devoted herself to the "realm of study, teaching, writing, speaking." But then she had "what is called nerve-wear by the patient and nervous prostration by the lookers-on."

Determined to recover, Frances Willard decided to learn how to ride the latest rage in America—the bicycle. She named her bicycle "Gladys" because of the "gladdening effect of its acquaintance and use on my health." At the time, bicycle riding by girls and women was very controversial. Various experts declared that bicycle riding would ruin the "fem-

Two young stenographers hold Frances Willard steady on Gladys.

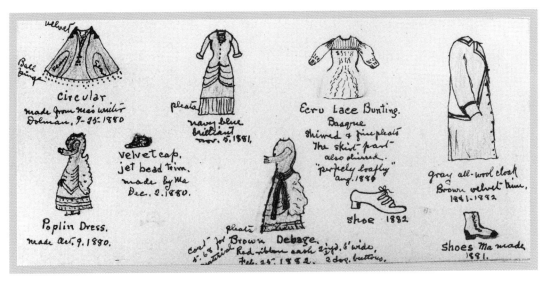

Sarah L. Gillispie made sketches of "a few of the dresses, etc. that Ma made for me for school."
Under each item, she wrote what it was and when her mother made it.

inine organs of matrimonial necessity," destroy "feminine symmetry and poise," and cause "bicycle eye" from raising the eyes while the head was lowered in a riding position. Other experts declared that bicycle riding was "good for girls, but bad for women." A Dr. J. West Roosevelt declared that bicycle riding was safe as long as "she does not over-exert herself by riding too long a time, or too fast, or up too steep hills." As for Willard, she published an essay, "How I Learned to Ride the Bicycle," and actively promoted the benefits of bicycle riding.

Bicycle riding brought about some long-overdue changes in fashion as female bicycle riders put on short skirts or bloomers and shed their stiff corsets, or, at least, wore lighter-weight versions. Bicycle riding also gave girls a way to have more freedom than they usually had. A popular song of the time, "Queen of the Bicycle Girls," included the lyrics:

> She is the Queen of the Bicycle Girls!
> She is the Queen of the Bicycle Girls!
> Cool as an icicle, when on her bicycle,
> She down the boulevard whirls.

Bicycle riding was not the only thing that girls were doing during this time. They were drinking newly invented ice-cream sodas, preparing picnic baskets to be raffled off at church socials, taking family trips on the rapidly expanding railroad lines that were crisscrossing the country, keeping autograph albums, gathering around the front parlor piano with their friends, and singing popular songs. They were also taking up another new sport—roller skating.

Minnie Radcliffe Douglas began roller skating when she was six years old. A year later she was performing in cities throughout America. She earned $15 a show and received rave reviews—"dazzling," "astonishing capabilities," and "the finest skatist in the land." She danced on skates and did tricks, including weaving around twelve burning torches that were set in a row eighteen inches apart. Minnie won the Sporting World's Medal. When she was eight years old, she retired and returned to school.

In the 1880s, a new wave of immigrants started arriving, including Italians, Bohemians, Hungarians, Greeks, Chinese, and Mexicans, who brought new languages, religions, and cultures to America. Hilda Satt, a Jewish girl from Poland, came with her family to

Minnie Radcliffe Douglas

Chicago, Illinois, in 1892, when she was nine years old. The following year, the Columbian Exposition, a huge fair, opened in Chicago.

"My father decided to take a day off from his work to take us to the fair," Hilda Satt Polacheck (her married name) later wrote. "We were speechless with excitement. The fair was a world of enchantments to us. The great Ferris wheel was shown here for the first time. When you got to the top you could almost touch the sky, we thought. I saw a diver for the first time and wondered how it was possible that he could stay underwater as long as he did—all of five minutes. . . . Greater thrills were still to come. As the light was fading in the sky, millions of lights were suddenly flashed on, all at one time. Having seen nothing but kerosene lamps for illumination, this was like getting a sudden vision of Heaven. Father marveled as much as we did. He told us that all these lights had been turned on with switches.

'Without matches?' I asked.

'Without matches,' he said.

'Just like the stars,' I said.

'The wonders of America are as wonderful as the stars,' he said with great reverence."

Hilda Satt Polacheck as a young girl.

While many girls were benefiting from the wonders of America, other girls were not. Many immigrant girls—Italian, Bohemian, Hungarian—

worked very long hours for very little pay. Orphan girls wandered the streets of big cities. Some Chinese girls were being bought in China and sent to be prostitutes in America. One former prostitute in San Francisco, Lilac Chen, later recalled how she had been sold in China when she was six years old: "My own father, imagine, . . . sold me on the ferry boat. Locked me in the cabin while he was negotiating my sale."

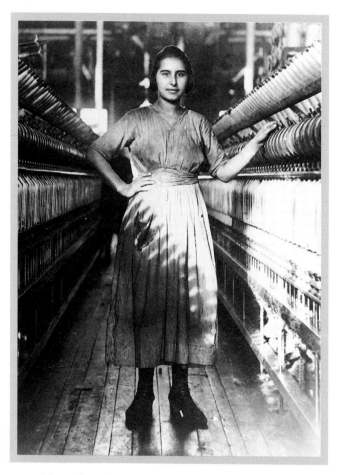

Maria Tomacchio at age fifteen. An Italian immigrant, Maria worked in the spinning room of a mill in Lawrence, Massachusetts.

Conditions for black people in America were dramatically deteriorating, particularly in the southern states. The last federal troops that had been stationed in the South were withdrawn in 1877, and the period known as Reconstruction ended. Violence against black people increased, including lynchings. State and local laws were passed, known as Jim Crow laws, to keep black and white people apart. Black people were forced to go to separate schools, ride in the backs of streetcars, live in separate neighborhoods, and stay out of parks that were designated for "whites only."

Native Americans had been finally overwhelmed by the avalanche of settlers and the military force and policies of the U.S. government. Indians were now forced to live on reservations. Zitkala-Ša, or Red Bird, also known as Gertrude Simmons Bonnin, was born on a reservation in South Dakota. Red Bird, who grew up to be an author and reformer, was sent away to a school run by white Quaker missionaries in Indiana when she was eight years old. Later, she wrote about an incident that happened at the school: "Late in the morning, my friend Judewin gave me a terrible warning. Judewin knew a few words of English and she had overheard the

Indian students at Santa Fe Indian school. The dolls and miniature furniture and appliances were used to train the girls to work for white families.

Hopi girls with squash–blossom hair styles, the symbol that they are ready for marriage.
Each girl had proven her mastery of domestic skills by grinding corn for four days
in a darkened room.

paleface woman talk about cutting our long, heavy hair. Our mothers taught us that only unskilled warriors who were captured had their hair shingled by the enemy. Among our people, short hair was worn by the mourners, and shingled hair by cowards! . . . 'No, I will not submit! I will struggle first!' I answered."

Red Bird slipped away, crawled under the bed, and curled up in a dark corner. As she hid and listened, Red Bird realized that all the women and girls, even Judewin, were looking for her. In time, they found her. Although she kicked and scratched, she was soon tied in a chair. "I cried aloud, shaking my head all the while until I felt the cold blades of the scissors against my neck, and heard them gnaw off one of my thick braids. Then I lost my spirit. Since the day I was taken from my mother I had suffered extreme indignities. People had stared at me. I had been tossed about in the air like a wooden puppet. And now my long hair was shingled like a coward's! In my anguish I moaned for my mother, but no one came to comfort me. Not a soul reasoned quietly with me, as my own mother used to do; now I was only one of many little animals driven by a herder."

Two Zuni girls standing beside a pueblo building.

In time, Red Bird got her revenge when she was told to mash turnips for dinner. "With fire in my heart, I took the wooden tool that the paleface woman held out to me. I stood upon a step, and grasping the handle with both hands, I bent in hot rage over the turnips [that were in a jar]. I worked my vengeance upon them." She mashed the turnips so hard that the bottom of the jar broke—although the woman did not know it until she picked up the jar and the turnips splattered all over the floor. "She spared me no scolding phrases that I had earned. I did not heed them. I felt triumphant in my revenge, though deep within me I was a wee bit sorry to have broken the jar," Red Bird later wrote. "As I sat eating my dinner, and I saw that no turnips were served, I whooped in my heart for having once asserted the rebellion within me."

As the nineteenth century came to a close, one woman said in 1893, "The world moves. Forty years ago how very little was known of women in public life. . . . Forty years ago only a very few, even of women themselves, believed in her equal rights with men before the law, let alone her open acknowledgment of any such sentiment. Today she is everywhere except in Congress and State Legislatures. A lawyer, doctor, minister, typewriter, stenographer, can run steam boats or a cattle ranch, tend switches, despatch trains or talk by lightning [telephone]."

The daughter of a fish dealer who worked with her father in Chinatown in San Francisco, California.

Clearly the world had moved. Girls growing up at the end of the nineteenth century had unprecedented opportunities. None of the opportunities had come easily or without controversy or without the efforts of countless numbers of determined and insistent girls. Girls such as Susan La Flesche Picotte, who was born on a

The four Crisman sisters were homesteaders. Each one staked out her own claim, built a shelter, and survived on the prairie.

reservation and grew up to become the first Native American woman physician and an advocate for Indian rights; Emma Goldman, who emigrated from Russia when she was sixteen and fought for free speech and birth control; Sarah Breedlove, who was orphaned when she was seven years old and grew up to become Madam C. J. Walker and build a business empire; and Elizabeth Jane "Pink" Cochran, who got a job with a newspaper when she wrote an indignant response to

Frances Perkins at age four. Perkins grew up to become the first woman in the U.S. cabinet. She was the architect of far-reaching reforms such as the minimum wage law and the Social Security Act.

an article that questioned what girls were good for.

Cochran, who became famous as Nellie Bly, would grow up to write about the lives of "working girls" and the conditions in "insane asylums" and jails. In 1890, she wrote newspaper articles and set a world record as she traveled around the world by ship, train, rickshaw, and tugboat in seventy-two days, six hours, and eleven minutes.

"When [I was] a very little girl," Cochran once recalled, "[I] wrote love and fairy stories by the score. On the flyleaves of books and on loose scraps of paper. For whole hours at night [I] lay in bed unable to go to sleep, . . . weaving tales and creating heroes and heroines."

8

"Prize It!"

GIRLS IN THE EARLY TWENTIETH CENTURY

Alice Sue Fun grew up in San Francisco's Chinatown in the early 1900s. Alice was seven years old when the 1906 earthquake and fire destroyed most of San Francisco. In the aftermath, she and her family lived in a makeshift tent. During that time, her father died of typhoid fever. The next year, Alice's mother got remarried to a man who worked as a cook. Her mother earned money by sewing at home.

Alice was raised to follow Chinese traditions. Her mother, like most Chinatown mothers, taught her to follow the "three obediences and four virtues" that were prescribed by Confucian ideology. The three obediences were to obey her father at home, obey her husband after marriage, and obey her eldest son when widowed. The four virtues were: propriety in behavior, speech,

Alice Sue Fun, with her uncle, her mother, and her siblings. Alice is standing next to her uncle.

demeanor, and household duties. At home, Alice and her family spoke Chinese, ate Chinese food, learned Chinese culture, and celebrated Chinese holidays. They worshipped Chinese gods, brewed Chinese herbs to cure ailments, and told legends and stories, including scary ghost stories. They also attended the Chinese opera. According to Alice, "In the old days, there were two operas a day. . . . Everyone ate and talked during the opera. It was quite festive. That's how I learned to love the opera."

During her growing up, Alice attended the Oriental Public School from 9:00 to 2:30 and True Sunshine Chinese School from 2:30 to 5:00. After school, she did household chores and watched her younger brothers and sisters. "I was the one who sewed their clothes, using those old foot treadle machines. Everything was used. I would take an old shirt apart and repiece it together for Little Brother's trousers," she later recalled.

During her girlhood, Alice did not have much freedom, because "Mother watched us like a hawk. We couldn't move without telling her. When we were growing up, we were never allowed to go out unless accompanied by an older brother, sister, or somebody else. . . . If you wanted to go shopping, you might as well forget it because, one thing, you didn't have any money. Secondly, you knew your mother wouldn't let you go, so what's the use of asking, right?"

Alice's school education ended when she was fifteen because it was time for her to go to work full-time and contribute money to her family. Although she gave half her pay to her mother, the amount she kept gave her a taste of independence. Before long, she got married and moved to New York, despite her mother's objections. Her marriage did not last long and she left New York to travel around the world as a maid and companion to the actress Lola Fisher. Alice lived a very different life than that of her mother. "My mother lived a very sheltered life," Alice explained. "Even up to her old age, she never trusted herself to go out alone. . . . I would go out anytime I want and anywhere I want."

Alice Sue Fun was part of the first generation of girls who grew up in the twentieth century, a century of dramatic, challenging, and exhilarating changes.

During the early years of the twentieth century, the first successful airplane was invented and built. Automobiles became a more common sight. Transatlantic communication became possible. Child labor was legal and

Hazel (back), Helen (sitting), Genevieve (right), and Kenneth (left) McVey grew up in Boulder, Colorado.

hundreds of thousands of youngsters worked in factories, mines, and mills. According to one woman who had gone to work as a child in 1901, "The corner of a shop would resemble a kindergarten because we were young, eight, nine, ten years old."

A new type of store, a department store, was established: Macy's in New York City, Filene's in Boston, and Nordstrom in Seattle, Washington. The first comics appeared in newspapers, including comic strips called "Dolly Dingle" and "Sally Slick and her Surprising Aunt Amelia." The first movie theaters, known as nickelodeons, were opening everywhere. Hilda Satt Polacheck later described how she ran errands until she earned a nickel so she could go to the first nickelodeon in Chicago. "I recall that it was not considered 'nice' to go. . . . So without telling Mother or anybody else, my best pal and I sort of sneaked into the show."

According to Hilda, "The place had been a small store. At one end was the screen. . . . There were rickety folding chairs set up and an ancient piano. . . . Soon the lights were dimmed, and after some 'oohing and aaahing' on the part of the audience . . . the piano began to play and

A little girl worker in a textile factory.

A fashionable girl who grew up in San Francisco.

Salanne Cuthbert holding a Japanese doll.

Cover (left) and title page illustration (right) of
Betty Gordon in the Land of Oil *published in 1920.*

objects began to move across the screen. Was it possible for a horse and wagon to move? . . . But here it was, before our very eyes. And then, wonder of wonders, a fire engine raced across."

During this period, a wide variety of books aimed at girls were published. Fiction books appeared with engaging girl characters such as *Rebecca of Sunnybrook Farm* by Kate Douglass Wiggins. Series books with fun-loving, adventurous girls were published, such as the Dorothy Dale series by Margaret Penrose, which included *Dorothy Dale's Strange Discovery* and *Dorothy Dale to the Rescue*. Biographies by famous women were very popular, includ-

*Helen Keller (left)
with her teacher,
Annie Sullivan.*

ing *The Story of My Life* by Helen Keller. A famous writer and speaker, Keller had been both deaf and blind from early childhood.

As for what girls read in school, Dorothy Marie Johnson, who was called Marie, later recalled, "Our school readers stressed literature of bygone days. Authors were men with beards, except Edgar Allan Poe had a little mustache."

Marie grew up in Whitefish, Montana. "Our house, unlike many, was painted on the outside, papered on the inside with fashionable dark reds and greens that swallowed up the lamplight. We had three rooms: front room, bedroom and kitchen . . . with no plumbing. . . . The water supply was wherever one chose to keep the pail and the dipper," she remembered.

Students and their teacher in front of their sod schoolhouse.

According to Marie, "We didn't have playground equipment at school; we didn't need it. For a few years, there was a vacant lot, still wild. Little girls could bend down a sarvisberry branch for a door and have an imaginary house. Boys tried to sneak across the street to watch Mr. Parent shoe horses. They were not supposed to bother him. I . . . sneaked, too."

Marie recalled that "boys played ball if they had a ball. Girls jumped rope if they had a rope. As we grew, a time came when boys sometimes jumped rope with us, to prove they could, not admitting they liked to be around girls. We turned the rope Pepper and Red Hot Pepper for especially exuberant boys until they got their big feet tangled and went down laughing."

Marie was twelve when the United States entered World War I in 1917. She later recalled, "Food shortages and economies we could put up with, and colors that ran because no more dyes came from Germany, but Uncle George was Over There, and I was worried. He wrote awfully good letters. The first time I ever saw the word *morale*, it was in his handwriting." During the war, the government sold Liberty Bonds to help pay for the war. Marie decided to buy one for fifty dollars. She later recalled, "I counted my assets; cash on hand and the nickel-and-dime savings of a twelve-year lifetime came to $47.10. I decided to shoot the works. My mother . . . lent me the necessary $2.90 without interest to make up the total."

The war ended shortly after Marie bought her bond, so she decided that "the Kaiser, informed by German Intelligence that the little John-

Ruth Gill grew up in the early twentieth century in Fort McDowell, Arizona.

son girl in Whitefish, Montana, had bought a Liberty Bond . . . heaved his spiked helmet through a window of his palace [and gave up]. The Armistice was signed November 11, 1918. And Uncle George came back and married Miss Huntington, who had been my fourth-grade teacher."

During the early twentieth century, girls grew up in a variety of sit-

Clothes hanging out to dry between rows of apartment buildings in New York City, in 1939.

uations. Kate Simon grew up in an apartment, "a top-floor railroad flat, with most of the rooms strung off a long hall" with "an indoor toi-let all our own" in the Bronx, New York. Edith Gallo was growing up in a coal mining camp near Cen-terville, Iowa. "I was born one cold December night," she later recalled. "I was placed in a large shoe box all lined with cotton, and set in back of the coal stove. I was kept there, cleaned and fed, until I became a little stronger. . . . All the homes in this mining camp had four rooms. . . . Within these four rooms lived my father, mother, three boys, and four girls."

Paik Kuang Sun, who was born in Korea and came to America when she was six years old, was growing up in Riverside, California, in a small one-room shack with her parents and siblings, including her older brother Meung. "Every Saturday Meung and I went to the slaughterhouse some distance away to get the animal organs that the butcher threw out:

pork and beef livers, hearts, kidneys, entrails, and tripe—all the things they considered unfit for human consumption. We were not alone—Filipino and Mexican children came there also. They needed those things to survive just as we did. The butchers stood around laughing at us as we scrambled for the choice pieces. When I told Father I didn't want to go there anymore because they were making fun of us, he said that we should thank God that they didn't know the value of what they threw out; otherwise we would go hungry." Paik, who later became known as Mary Paik Lee, recalled that she and Meung were always called "hey you" at school instead of by their Korean names. "I told Meung that it was too late to change our names but we should give American names to our siblings." In time, she and Meung convinced their parents to give the rest of their children American names—Ernest, Stanford, Ralph, Lawrence, and Charlotte.

Era Bell Thompson

Era Bell Thompson was growing up on a farm near Driscoll, North Dakota. Her family was one of the few black families in the state. According to Thompson, "Haying time, to me, was the happiest time of the year. . . . Our whole family took to the field. We arose early, while the air was still fresh and cool, before the sun was up. . . . My first job was driving a horse that was hitched to a device called a stacker. This implement lifted the hay up to the stack. When I had mastered this task, I was taught to drive the hayrake. . . . At noon we unhitched the horses, fed them, and sat down under the shade of the rake to eat . . . hard slices of summer sausage, potato salad, soupy with vinegar, hard-boiled eggs, bread, and buttermilk. Sometimes cookies. Brushing aside the flies that suddenly came out of nowhere, we ate steadily, silently, leaving nothing."

Alice Greenough

Alice Greenough grew up in Red Lodge, Montana. Her father, "Packsaddle Ben" Greenough, had grown up an orphan in Brooklyn, New York. Her mother grew up in Illinois, where she had helped her mother run a boardinghouse after her father died. Alice had seven brothers and sisters, including Frank and Marge. According to Alice, "He [her father] always had a lot of horses around—two, three hundred horses. A lot of them weren't even halter-broke. . . . He'd look at 'em and he'd say, 'Well, Frank, take this, Alice, you take that. And Marge, take that one.' One of his famous expressions was, 'If you can't ride 'em, walk.'

"We rode to school, we learned to drive teams, . . . learned to [back]pack in the mountains. . . . We'd go way up around Bear Tooth Lake. Then he'd go into the mountains for a month or so and leave us in the camp by ourselves with no living human closer than three days' trip horseback. . . . I don't think I was ever frightened. . . . He never left a gun with us. He left a fishhook and some line, and we fished. We killed grouse with a rock. I can't think of a day in those mountains that we didn't have fun. If nothing else, we'd have contests to see who'd catch the most fish. We'd see who could climb to the top of a mountain first. . . . We always found something to do."

Maria Margarita Obregon grew up in El Paso, Texas.

Andreita Padilla was raised by her grandmother in La Paloma, New Mexico. "She was an angel," Andreita later recalled. "I was very small—and, oh, she was big—big, with a round face, all red; green eyes and big eyelashes. . . . She was very, very poor. The floors of her house were made of *tierra* [earth], *soquete* [mud]. We had a cow, but my grandmother she didn't have nothing to buy food for the cow. So we used to cut alfalfa. She'd say, 'Let's go *mi'jita* [dear daughter].' We'd go over to the ditch and we'd cut some hay and grass and all kinds of weeds. Then we'd bring them for the cow to eat. We'd feed the cow, and all week we'd have milk. . . . We drank that milk with *galletas* [biscuits] in the morning, we drank that milk at noon with *galletas* or *tortillas*, we drank that milk at supper with *galletas* and with *sopa* [a type of bread pudding in New Mexico]. We used to eat *frijoles* [pinto beans] and *chile*, too, corn, if somebody gave her corn. But most of all we drank milk, milk."

When Andreita's grandmother died, she went to live with her other grandmother. "She was *sorda*, deaf, and she couldn't see right. . . . She kept me working all the time. On Mondays we had to wash. We brought the water in from outside. Even if there was snow. . . . We'd get the water in a bucket and we'd bring it inside and we'd put it in the tub. Then we'd start washing the clothes. We'd wash them and right away we'd take them over to the stove and boil them. Then we'd take them outside, wash them again and put in the bluing. First the cold water then the bluing. Oh! It was so clean and as pretty. . . . Then I'd hang it up. I was too small to do it, but she made me, and I did it.

"On Saturday . . . we washed our hair and we had our baths and we didn't use any soap at all. We used *amole*. It grows over there on the hills. We'd pick it for the root, . . . then we'd smash it with the hammer and put it in the sun to dry. When we washed our hair, we'd use it with water, like powder. It made a lot of lather, *espuma*, bubbles. We washed our hair in the tub and it came out shiny, shiny, beautiful."

Wherever they grew up, all girls had the experience of starting to menstruate. Andreita later recalled how it happened for her. "One Saturday—I remember I was about eleven or twelve—and *se empezó el tiempo* [I started my period]. I got really scared. I didn't know what was happening. I thought I was dying. We were eating dinner, and I knew after we started eating she'd never let me get up until I'd finished, but I felt something.

" '*Abuelita*, I have to go to the toilet, *excusado*.'

'How many times do I have to tell you when God's serving your food, you don't supposed to move.'

She was about to spank me, and I didn't know what to say. So I just said, 'Something's happening to me. . . . What happened?'

'Well, this is *tu tiempo* [your time].'

'What's *tiempo*?'

'Every lady has that. It's natural for every little girl when they get so many years. Some are thirteen, and some are ten. You don't have to worry.'

So I think, 'This is going to happen every month.'"

The early years of the twentieth century were a time that many historians call the "Progressive Era" because there were many reform movements. Throughout the decades, people worked to end child labor, expose dishonest politicians and businessmen, and improve the terrible living and working conditions that many people endured, especially immigrants who lived in cities.

Elizabeth Gurley Flynn joined the fight to end child labor and improve workers' lives when she was fifteen. She organized workers, participated in

Yedda Welled, Rebecca Cohen, and Rebecca Kerwin were papergirls in Hartford, Connecticut.

Margaret and Mildred Storey grew up in Prescott, Arizona.

strikes, and gave fiery speeches. According to one newspaper account, Elizabeth's "power of speech has won her spellbound audiences." Because of her activities, she spent time in jail. Joe Hill, a labor organizer and songwriter, wrote a popular song about Elizabeth Gurley Flynn, titled "Rebel Girl," that included these lyrics:

That's the Rebel Girl.
That's the Rebel Girl.
To the working class she's a
    precious pearl.

Margaret Sanger and Mary Ware Dennett spearheaded the movement to provide information about sex and birth control. Sanger wrote a magazine column, "What Every Girl Should Know," and covered topics such as pregnancy, masturbation, and menstruation. Mary Ware Dennett wrote a booklet, *The Sex Side of Life: An Explanation for Young People* that read in part, "When boys and girls get into their 'teens, a side of them begins to wake up which has been asleep or only partly developed ever since they were born, that is, the sex side of them. It is the most wonderful and interesting part of growing up. This waking is partly of the mind, partly of the body, and partly of the feelings or emotions."

Juliette Gordon Low, who was called Daisy, focused her energies on founding a new organization for girls. She began on March 12, 1912, by organizing eighteen girls in Savannah, Georgia, into a group that would become known as the Girl Scouts. "I've got something for the girls of Savannah, and all America, and all the world, and we're going to start it tonight," she told her cousin, Nina Pape.

The first Girl Scout uniform was a dark blue middy blouse and skirt and a light blue tie. Girls could earn a variety of proficiency badges by accomplishing a set of prescribed tasks. A Girl Scout who could demonstrate that she knew automobile mechanics, first aid, and how to drive could earn a driving badge, "Motorist." For the "Flyer" badge, the tasks included

Girl Scouts attending a scout rally in Central Park, New York City in 1920.

building an airplane that flew at least twenty-five yards. There were also Dairy Maid, Cook, and Laundress badges.

The struggle for women's suffrage, or the right to vote, intensified as a new generation of leaders took charge. Carrie Chapman Catt was president of the National American Woman Suffrage Association. Catt, who

Martha Gellhorn with her mother, Edna, and other suffragettes in St. Louis, Missouri.

was born Carrie Lane, grew up in Iowa. From an early age, she was good at figuring things out, including how to stop her brother, Charles, from chasing her with a snake. At first, Carrie screamed and ran away. But then one day, she realized that if the snake had not hurt Charles, it would not hurt her. A few days later, she picked up a snake, caught Charles by surprise, and wrapped the snake around his neck. Charles was terrified and never teased Carrie again.

Alice Paul, who grew up in New Jersey, was another key leader. At the age of sixteen, she went to college. As a young woman, she and her friend Lucy Burns founded the National Woman's Party and introduced militant activities, including huge suffrage parades.

Lucy Haessler went to parades with her mother. "I was only ten years old the first time I went to a march with my mother. She told me, 'Oh, you're too young, you can't go.' But I said, 'I *am* going, because you're going to win the right to vote and I'm going to vote when I'm grown-up.' So she let me march. . . . Everyone there was much older and bigger than me, and they took longer steps than I did. So I had to really hustle to keep up with my mother, but I managed to do it. Just like the other suffragettes, I wore a white blouse and skirt, and a purple and gold sash that came across my front. Purple and gold were the colors of the women's suffrage movement. . . . I was so excited."

In 1917, Alice Paul, Lucy Burns, and women of all ages started picketing the White House. Standing in silence, they held banners that read, HOW LONG MUST WOMEN WAIT FOR LIBERTY? Hundreds of women were arrested and charged with obstructing sidewalk traffic. More than a hundred women served time in jail. When sixteen jailed women went on a hunger strike, they were force-fed. "I was held down by five people at legs, arms, and head," Lucy Burns wrote on tiny scraps of paper that were smuggled out of the jail. As news of the suffragists' treatment spread, public pressure forced authorities to release them.

Finally, on August 26, 1920, 144 years after the Declaration of Independence was adopted, 133 years after the U.S. Constitution was ratified, and 72 years after the first women's rights convention was held at Seneca Falls, New York, the Nineteenth Amendment to the Constitution was ratified and women's suffrage was the law of the land. At the time, Lucille Thornburgh was twelve years old. She lived in Strawberry, Tennessee, twenty-two miles from Knoxville, a day's journey by horse and wagon. "We didn't hear about it right away," she later recalled. "We didn't have a telephone. We didn't have a radio. We didn't have electricity. We found out through the newspaper. It would come about one o'clock and most of the time it was a day or so late. My mother was real excited about it. She said well at last, at last, now we can vote. My mother voted right up until she died."

According to Carrie Chapman Catt, "The vote is the emblem of your equality, women of America, the guaranty of your liberty. . . . Women have suffered agony of soul . . . that you and your daughters might inherit political freedom. *That vote has been costly. Prize it!*"

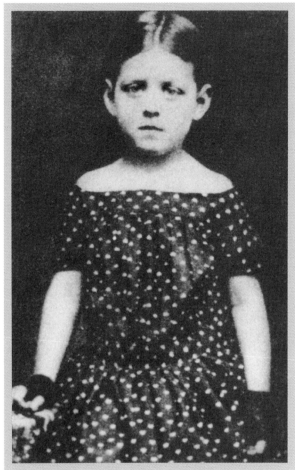

Carrie Chapman Catt at the age of six.

9

Changes and Challenges

GIRLS IN THE MID-TWENTIETH CENTURY

Yvonne "Eve" Blue was fourteen years old and living in Chicago when she started writing in her diary about her weight. "Three months in which to lose thirty pounds—but I'll do it—or die in the attempt," she wrote on July 3, 1926.

On July 11, she wrote, "I was so weak I could hardly pull myself out of bed. My hands shook terribly and I grew hot and cold by turns. I managed to dress, but when I went downstairs Mother said I looked so shakey and pale and sick that she *made* me eat. And to tell the truth I wasn't sorry, I had gone 60 hours without food."

On July 27, Eve wrote, "Mother and Daddy make me so mad! They *make* me eat. Last week I had an average of less than 140 calories a day and I lost 7 pounds. And now they won't let me

Yvonne Blue

diet. Last night I dropped most of the meat in my lap, rolled it in my napkin and fed it to Tar Baby [the cat] and at breakfast I put half my orange and bread in my napkin and threw it away later. I hate to do it, but what am I to do. I *won't* eat it."

Six months later, she wrote, "In Home Economics we are studying calories and Thursday we had to write down everything that we had eaten the previous day. Now as it happens I have been reducing for the past two weeks and my total number of calories for the day was but 635—a sum noticably in arrear of the recognized 2500. I told her [the teacher] I was attempting to make the ol' scales register a trifle less when I mounted them and the up-shot was that I was kept after class while she lectured. She told me:

1. That if I kept it up I'd die
2. That I was not too heavy
3. That thin girls weren't pretty
4. That I was so foolish about this when generally I was so 'honest' and 'sensible.' (heaven forbid)
5. That if I was really overweight, which she doubted, she'd help me reduce, but consume 1800 calories a day. She asked me why I wished to reduce and I told her because I felt better that way. She said that she didn't believe me—but it's true."

Eve's friends worried about their weight, too. Bobbie wanted "to be very thin." Mattie informed Eve that she had had a dream in which Eve "wore a lumberjack blouse and a checked skirt, and you were so thin I nearly died of envy. I am terribly fat."

Eve and her friends belonged to the first generation of girls who worried about being overweight—the first girls who wrote in their diaries about dieting. They were also the first generation of girls to grow up when the rapidly growing advertising industry was glorifying the slender, long-limbed, small-breasted female figure. In real life, the slender look was adopted by girls and young women who were known as flappers. The flapper look typically started with a haircut that was a dramatic change from the long hairstyles of the past. In her diary, Eve described getting such a haircut. "Yesterday I went to the barber's and had my hair shingle bobbed cut in a bob just like a boy's, only longer."

Flappers also tweezed their eyebrows, put on bright red lipstick, and wore short skirts. They drank and smoked cigarettes. They danced in marathons and used the "in" phrase "Boop Boop A Doop," from the cartoon character Betty Boop.

Many adults across America were horrified. "This part of the country

FLAPPER FANNY says

It isn't long before the first blush of youth is succeeded by the second blush of the drug store.

Flapper Fanny cartoon

[Tennessee] is called the Bible Belt, and everybody said that the flappers were going to hell," Lucille Thornburg remembered. "But girls did it anyway. My sisters and I sure did. We considered the skirts short, and they were just a couple of inches above our knees." Although she was a young girl in Huron, South Dakota, when her aunts came to visit, Bernice Stuart Snow never forgot that they came "with real short dresses above their knees, stockings rolled down beneath their knees, and high heels. They had the new hairdo. . . . They smoked cigarettes. . . . The town was scandalized. . . . You weren't considered a nice girl if you looked like that."

The decade of the 1920s was the time when many of the features of modern America took hold. Electricity was widely used for lighting, cooking, and household appliances. Consumer goods galore were being widely produced—refrigerators, automobiles, pianos—and widely advertised as never before. The cosmetic industry began to boom. New devices of mass media—radio and movies—were creating a mass culture by transmitting images, messages, and experiences to huge numbers of people in America.

More people were using telephones, although they were still considered a luxury in many parts of the country. Marie Johnson in Montana,

As supervisors stood behind them, telephone operators plugged wires into the switchboard to connect callers.

who got a job as a switchboard operator when she was fourteen, recalled that "not everybody had a telephone—at $1.74 a month on a four-party line, it was a luxury that lots of people could do without. . . . Teenagers didn't monopolize telephones. They hadn't thought of it. Most of them were half scared to use the telephone." In fact, the idea of being a teenager "hadn't even been invented back in the early 1920s," Marie explained. "There were just big kids, little kids, and babies."

Allison McCrillis, who was born at the beginning of the 1920s and grew up in Northampton, Massachusetts, later recalled that "four primary agents of change played an ever-increasing role in our lives: the radio, the movies, the automobile and the airplane. . . . The first radios that we children of the '20s remember were the so-called crystal sets consisting of a small wooden box with a cord and two sets of earphones. . . . The first partly talking picture, *The Jazz Singer*, opened . . . in 1928. . . . Perhaps the favorite film star of us little girls in the '20s was Janet Gaynor, who specialized in Cinderella roles that always led up to a happy ending."

Patti Jean Mount grew up in Zanesville, Ohio.

Old photographs show Allison and her friends in about 1924 "wearing long cotton stockings and bulky homemade frocks." However, by the end of the decade, she and her friends "were tearing around in ski pants in winter and shorts in the summer." As for their hair, the style for little

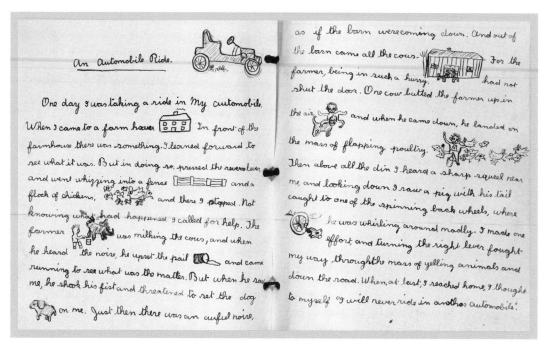

In about 1908, Mabel Hall Colgate wrote and illustrated "An Automobile Ride" in her story book. Mabel first drove a car at the age of thirteen.

girls was "the Dutch cut; short on the sides, shingled in the back, with bangs over the forehead."

Allison's father sold automobiles and their first car was "a used Overland touring car with a canvas top and heavy celluloid side-curtains that were snapped into place in case of rain." As the number of cars skyrocketed and more and more roads were built, Sunday afternoon drives became a popular pastime for many families. So did swimming. "We all wore heavy wool-jersey suits with 'modesty skirts' around the hips of women's and girls' suits. Some bathers wore rubber caps and bathing-slippers as well," Allison recalled.

By the late 1920s, Allison and her family "were quite accustomed . . . to seeing and hearing small airplanes circling above our town, and indeed occasional entrepreneurs landed in the meadow on the Holyoke road to take passengers up for $5." Still, they were dazzled when they attended "the great Air Meet" and saw "all the wonders of modern aviation, from barnstorming to commercial flying and military demonstrations. . . . Aviatrix Maud Tait landed in her Commandaire to represent the ladies, and Gladys Johnson, aged 18, made a parachute jump."

The 1920s ended with a disaster when, in 1929, the stock market crashed. According to Allison, "On Oct. 29, the day of the great Stock

The daughter of a migrant auto worker doing her homework in her tent home in Corpus Christi, Texas, during the Great Depression.

A girl standing in the doorway of her home in Sebastin, Texas, in the 1930s.

Market crash, our Gazette [newspaper] that evening bore a large black headline: 'STOCK PRICES TUMBLE IN STORM SELLING.' . . . It took quite some time for everybody to absorb what had happened and to give it a name: The Depression. We kids were to grow up in it through the '30s. . . . A popular song of the 1920s, 'My God, How the Money Rolls In,' was replaced by the song, 'Brother, Can You Spare A Dime?'"

The Great Depression lasted throughout the 1930s. Banks closed their doors. Factories and mills shut down. Millions and millions of people lost their jobs. Farmers lost their farms. Some parts of the country were hit harder than others. So were some people. "'Use it up; wear it out; make it do; and go without' became a way of life for us all," Allison later wrote. Evelyn Fairbanks, who lived on Rondo Avenue in the black neighborhood in St. Paul, Minnesota, remembered that "paper, wood, and cardboard were fuel. Fish scales and guts were buried to fertilize the

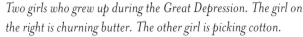
Two girls who grew up during the Great Depression. The girl on the right is churning butter. The other girl is picking cotton.

garden. Coffee grounds were sprinkled over the fishing worm bed and then covered with a staked-down gunnysack." Jessie Lopez de la Cruz, who was ten years old when the Depression began and the daughter of migrant workers in California, remembered that "during the Depression . . . I didn't have a sweater. I had nothing. I'd come to school and they'd want to know, 'What did you have for breakfast?' They gave us paper, to write down what we had! I *invented* things! We had eggs and milk, I'd say."

Like many girls, Jessie helped her family survive. She worked in the fields. "I used to lift a 12-foot sack of cotton with 104 or 112 pounds," Jessie explained. "I could get that sack and put it on my shoulder, and walk . . . to where the scale was. I could hook this sack up on the scale, have it weighed, take it off the hook and put it back on my shoulder and walk up a ladder about eight feet high and dump all that cotton in the trailer."

Jade Snow Wong, who was eight years old and living in San Francisco, later recalled, "Daddy faced the grim times with Mama. They were explor-

In Melrose, Louisiana, two sisters walk home with some fish for their family.

ing ways for more severe economy, and in their discussion, Mama said, 'Jade Snow is old enough to take over my housework so that I can do as much sewing as possible. Perhaps you can go out and solicit odd work which I can do at home. It is time for our daughter to learn the meaning of money, the necessity for thrift, and how to keep house.'"

Elizabeth Zofchak, who was thirteen at the time, her parents, and seven brothers and sisters lived in East Akron, Ohio. "The neighborhood was Slovaks, Ukrainians, Russians, and Polish. Some black families who worked at Goodyear lived there, too," she later explained. "We weren't allowed to speak English [they spoke Slovak] at home. My father said, 'When you're in school, you can learn.'"

When the Depression began, her father leased a coal mine near Talmadge, Ohio. Elizabeth later recalled, "It was a small mine under a big hill. . . . My father took me to work in the mine dressed up like a boy. . . . I wore shoes like the Boy Scouts, with a little knife in the side. . . . I liked going off to the mine in boys' clothes, with my hair cut short. It made me feel good to know I could help the family. . . . Before we went in, my father would set his pick upright and lay his leather cap over it. We knelt down on the dirt while he said a prayer in Slovak to ask God to protect us underground. We would repeat the prayer word for word. He'd do the same thing at the end of the day, to give thanks that we had come out safely. . . . We dug coal to buy flour, salt, sugar, and other essentials. . . . We'd trade coal . . . for groceries. . . . My father could have gotten arrested for having a girl in the mine, but I never got caught."

A little girl at an Indian Nursery School, Nette Lake Kochiching, in Nette Lake, Minnesota.

Despite the hard times, movies were enormously popular during the Great Depression. Throughout the 1930s, there were an estimated eighty-five million paid admissions a week. Children under the age of twelve paid ten cents. For that they saw a newsreel; a "short subject" or a two-reel comedy; then the B picture, a low-budget film in black and white; and

Shirley Temple

finally the feature film. Shirley Temple, who was born the year the stock market crashed, was a big star by the time she was three years old. Many girls imitated Shirley Temple by learning to tap dance, wearing their hair in corkscrew curls, and singing "On the Good Ship Lollipop."

Allison McCrillis and her friends were avid moviegoers. "The movies provided us with an inexpensive escape from the grimness of the Depression days and also probably affected our values as well," Allison recalled. "Certainly we learned that smoking and drinking signify sophistication; that crime does not pay; that money cannot buy happiness; . . . that women want marriage over careers in the long run; . . . that good cowboys wear white hats; and that the butler probably did it."

Allison and her friends also loved newspaper comic strips, including "Ella Cinders." "We girls loved Ella for her grit and her ability to outwit all the villains who beset her," she later explained. Like everyone else, they listened to many different radio programs, including *Little Orphan Annie*, *The Lone Ranger*, and *Buck Rogers*. A particularly favorite program was *The Shadow*. Allison and her friends loved to show off their version of The Shadow's "fiendish laugh and his warning that 'The Shadow Knowwwwwws.'"

In the 1940s, these two girls attended a summer camp and found a great spot for reading.

In 1941, the United States entered World War II after Japanese pilots bombed the U.S. naval base at Pearl Harbor. "I was about eight when I heard the announcements of war starting," recalled Hannah Mason, who was living in New Jersey. "I remember hearing Roosevelt's [President Franklin Roosevelt] voice on the radio and our family listening, and then the newsreels at the movie showed what happened."

The need for extraordinary amounts of war materiel kicked the economy into high gear and the Great Depression finally ended. As millions of men joined the military, millions of women went to work doing jobs that had been closed to women until the war began. Girls pitched in to help the war effort in a variety of ways. They saved and salvaged newspapers, rags, scrap metal, flattened aluminum and tin cans,

A shipyard worker in Orange, Texas, picking up her daughter from a nursery school.

rubber, nylon, and silk stockings. They bought war bonds and watched for spies because the government frequently sent out warnings. They planted and weeded vegetables in victory gardens and knitted squares to make afghans that the Red Cross distributed.

"The girls in our sixth grade were taught to knit six-inch squares, which the teacher sewed together to make afghans to be sent to the wounded soldiers," Evelyn Fairbanks recalled. "I won the prize for furnishing the most squares for the afghans. School prizes were always writing tablets, which were highly valued by the stu-

Girl Scouts and their leader gather scrap metal to help the war effort.

dents. The cost of the tablet—a nickel—was not a small sum to parents."

Girls wrote letters. Six-year-old Ruth Erling of Pennock, Minnesota, wrote to her father, who was a Marine in the South Pacific:

Dear Daddy

I got a loose tooth. We have only 10 pages left in our reading books. Helen tried to pull my tooth. We read about Pinocchio. We are all lonesome for you. I like the letter we got today.

Love, Ruth

Thirteen-year-old Charmaine Leavitt of Kalamazoo, Michigan, wrote to her next-door neighbor Justin Slager, who was in the army in North Africa.

Dear Justin,

. . . The other night I went to a Girl Scout Party. We went on a scavenger hunt. I had to get a cigar butt, 3 cups of mud, a girl's finger nail, a picture of Bob Hope and a couple of other things.

In school this year I am taking Latin, Jr. Business, Civics, English, Science, and Gym. And I don't like any of them. . . .

Your dog sure looks lonely, all he ever does is to sit on your front porch . . .

Sincerely Yours, Charmaine

One group of Americans—Japanese Americans—were excluded from joining the war effort. By order of President Franklin Roosevelt, and with the support of Congress, 110,000 Japanese Americans from the West Coast were forced to leave their homes and confined in camps.

While they were held at an internment camp in Heart Mountain, Wyoming, some Japanese-American girls took a class in judo. This young girl threw the male instructor.

The camps were surrounded by barbed wire and guarded by armed soldiers. "We were in the camp for the duration of the war," Barbara Aoki later recalled. "I started nursery school and went to second grade there."

The generation of girls who grew up during World War II were the first girls to see Wonder Woman, the first action heroine who was dressed in a costume. Wonder Woman was created by a man and introduced in a comic book in 1941. Gloria Steinem, who grew up to be a leader for women's rights, was seven years old when Wonder Woman appeared. Gloria was thrilled because the comic strip showed Wonder Woman battling evil men who "in the end, . . . are brought to their knees and made to recognize women's strength."

Girls who grew up during World War II grew up at a time when the media, radio, movies, newsreels, magazine articles, advertisements, posters, and photographs advertised a vast array of nontraditional jobs for women—riveter, welder, police officer, truck driver, and pilot. The words "woman power" were frequently used.

All that changed, however, when the war ended in 1945. Returning servicemen took back their jobs and many women returned to traditionally female jobs in clerical, sales, and domestic work. Although some other jobs were opening up for women as nurses, librarians, and teachers, now the media advertised the importance of women as wives and mothers. A new magazine called *Seventeen* spread this message to girls.

Brett Harvey recalled that she grew up after the war and read articles in *Seventeen* with titles such as "How to Be a Woman." In that article, young readers like Brett read, "There is no office, lab, or stage that offers so many creative avenues or executive opportunities as that everyday place, the home. . . . What profession offers the daily joy of turning out a delicious dinner, of converting a few yards of fabric, a pot of paint, and imagination into a new room? Of seeing a tired and unsure man at the end of a working day become a rested lord of his manor?"

Drew Gilpin Faust grew up in Virginia hearing her mother tell her, "It's a man's world, sweetie, and the sooner you learn that the better off you'll be." Drew, however, "responded to this instruction by refusing to

The author, in 1949, at the age of five. Except for the socks and shoes, her outfit is completely Moravian. Her mother, who dressed her, grew up in a part of Eastern Europe that is now the Czech Republic.

Girls and a boy playing "ring around a rosie" in Chicago, Illinois.

wear dresses and by joining the 4-H club, not to sew and can like all the other girls, but to raise sheep and cattle with the boys."

During the 1950s, life changed dramatically in America. Television replaced radio as the main medium. Suburbs mushroomed across the country and many girls found themselves living in identical-looking houses on the outskirts of cities and towns. The economy boomed and more families than ever before had more money than ever before. A slew of new consumer goods were produced—air conditioners, frozen foods, and fitted bed sheets—and manufacturers greatly increased the amount of money they spent on advertising. Consumers were urged to buy, buy, buy. A typical advertisement featured an attractive young wife and mother demonstrating a product. Increasing numbers of young women college students dropped out before graduating. Many quit to get married. Others dropped out because of the prevailing belief that having a B.A. (bachelor of arts degree) made a woman seem too smart and hurt her chances of getting a more important degree, a "Mrs."

"Tomboy" was a comic that appeared for a short time during the 1950s.

Voluptuous movie stars such as Marilyn Monroe were popular and big breasts became the rage. A big-busted doll—Barbie—was introduced. A new line of junior bras was designed just for girls. Department stores opened specialty shops with trained fitters to help first-time bra buyers. Many girls exercised by bending their elbows, clenching their fists, and pushing their arms back and forth while chanting:

> I must, I must, I must.
> I must develop my bust.

By the end of the 1950s, a vaccine was discovered for polio, a disease that had crippled tens of thousands of children each year. Hula hoops came and went. Jackie Ormes created the comic character "Patty Jo," a little African-American girl also manufactured as a doll, perhaps the first black character doll in America. A disc jockey coined the term "rock 'n' roll," and music that grew out of the African American blues tradition became the rage. Elvis Presley was a star. All-girl singing groups like the Bobbettes and Chantels were popular and inspired four black teenage girls in Passaic, New Jersey, to form the Shirelles.

Girls doing the twist in St. Paul, Minnesota.

The Shirelles first performed in school. In 1960, they became the first all-girl group to top the singles chart, with "Will You Still Love Me Tomorrow." As a teenager in the early 1960s, Susan Douglas listened to the Shirelles and other girl groups. According to Susan, music made her and her friends "feel a kind of euphoria that convinces us that we can transcend the shackles of conventional life."

Although the U.S. Supreme Court ruled in 1954 that segregation in public schools was unconstitutional, segregation remained entrenched throughout America.

In the South, laws known as Jim Crow laws enforced segregation in every aspect of life, including in parks, public transportation, drinking fountains, restaurants, and movie theaters. In the North, segregation was manifested in other ways. In some areas, real estate agents steered African-American home buyers away from white neighborhoods and

doctor in Tampa. On the way
on the bus we saw a sign
. Florida State Law
Colored passengers will sit
from the rear to the front of
the coach.
White passengers will sit
from the front to the rear of
the coach.
the afternoon we went swimm
the Sulfer Springs Pool. The wate

On her first trip to the South in 1956, fourteen-year-old Linda Hickson copied in her travel journal this sign, which she saw in a bus in Tampa, Florida.

towns. When African Americans did move into white neighborhoods, they frequently had to deal with isolation, vandalism, and violence.

Claudette Colvin grew up in Montgomery, Alabama, where because she was African American she was prohibited from doing many things. "My first anger I remember was when I wanted to go to the rodeo," Claudette said. "Daddy bought my sister boots and bought us both cowboy hats. That's as much of the rodeo as we got. The show was . . . only for white kids." Claudette "hated segregation" and she "was always rebellious." She did not accept her mother's explanation that "this is the way it is. The white people, they own everything, they bought everything, they built it."

In March of 1955, Claudette, who was fifteen years old then, was arrested in Montgomery for refusing to give up her seat on a bus to a white person. A police officer boarded the bus to get her to move, but Claudette refused. "I said, 'No, I do not have to get up. I paid my fare. . . . It's my constitutional right!'" Claudette later recalled. "The words just came into my mind. That history teacher and that literature teacher, they were just pricking our minds." Claudette was forcibly removed from the bus, handcuffed, arrested for violating the city segregation laws, and put in jail. She stayed there until she was bailed out. Then she was fined. Eleven months later, Rosa Parks also refused to give up her seat on a bus to a white person. Her arrest triggered the Montgomery bus boycott, which many people cite as the start of the modern civil rights movement.

By the mid-1960s, the struggle for civil rights had intensified and girls were in the middle of the action.

10

Unprecedented Possibilities

GIRLS APPROACHING THE MILLENNIUM

Sheyann Webb was named for her great-great-grandmother, who had been a slave. According to Sheyann, most people called her "Shey," and to pronounce it right, she said, "You drop the 'e' so it sounds like shy." Shey lived in Selma, Alabama, and her good friend Rachel West lived next door to her.

On January 11, 1965, Shey, who was eight years old, was walking to school when she saw people standing outside the Brown Chapel African Methodist Episcopal Church. The week before, Shey had heard Dr. Martin Luther King, Jr., speaking in her church about leading marches and seeking freedom for black people. "I knew something was going to happen. People had been coming and going around the apartments for several days," Shey recalled.

Shey went inside the church instead of going on to school. She listened to a man talk about how few black people had been able to register to vote. "If you can't vote," Shey heard the man say, "then you're not free. . . . you're a slave." She finally got to school around one o'clock.

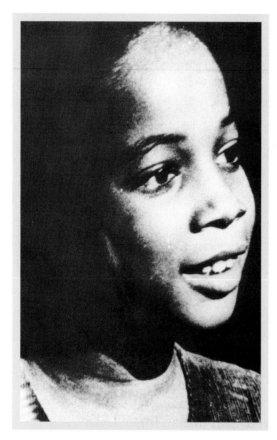

Shey Webb

When she told the teacher why she was late, the teacher said, "Don't you know what kind of meeting they're having over there? That's a voting-rights meeting, child. That's not for children like you. Don't you know there might be trouble—might be folks put in jail? You want to be put in jail?"

Shey told her mother about missing school and going to the meeting. Her mother warned Shey that the civil rights demonstrations could be dangerous. But Shey kept going to the meetings. "I would be the only child there," she later recalled. "I'd sit in back and listen. I hadn't told my mother and father about missing school." Rachel went, too, sometimes.

Shey's parents got involved after she told her mother that all she wanted for her ninth birthday present was for "her and Daddy to join the marches and try to register."

Whenever there was a gathering, there was always lots of singing. "Those songs carried a message. . . . Freedom songs cried out for justice right now, not later," Shey explained.

On Sunday, March 7, 1965, Shey went alone to join a group of people who were going to march across the Edmund Pettus Bridge in downtown Selma. Waiting on the other side were lines of state troopers and Sheriff Jim Clark with his deputies mounted on horses. The troopers had clubs in their hands and gas masks on their faces. "*That* scared me. I had never faced the troopers before, and nobody had ever put on gas masks during the downtown marches," Shey said later.

When the marchers in the front of the line reached the troopers, Shey heard a voice saying, "Troopers advance and see that they are dispersed." Swinging their clubs and setting off tear gas canisters, the troopers charged. The horsemen charged, too. "They rode right through the cloud of tear gas," Shey later recalled. "Some of them had clubs, others had ropes or whips, which they swung about them like they were driving cattle. . . . I heard the swish sound as the whip went over my head. . . . They kept rolling canisters of tear gas on the ground, so it would rise up quickly. It was making me sick. I heard more horses and I turned back and saw two of them and the riders were leaning over to one side. It was like a nightmare seeing it though the tears."

Shey ran all the way home. Her mother held her in her arms. That night, she sat with her friend Rachel in the front of Brown Chapel. People were in shock. Many were stunned and moaning, their eyes swollen and burning from the tear gas. But later in the night, suddenly somebody started humming. "I think they were moaning and it just went into the humming of a freedom song. It was real low, but some of us children began humming along, slow and soft. . . . It started to swell, the humming. Then we began singing the words. We sang, 'Ain't gonna let Jim Clark turn me 'round. Ain't gonna let no state trooper turn me 'round. . . . Ain't gonna let no horses . . . ain't gonna let no tear gas—

ain't gonna let nobody turn me 'round. *Nobody!*' "

Television cameras had recorded the attack on the marchers, and television viewers all over the country watched in horror. The day would become known as Bloody Sunday. The next day, Martin Luther King, Jr., and people from all over, came to Selma, and two days later about two thousand people, including Shey, marched across the bridge. This time the troopers stood back.

"If I live to be a hundred-and-three, I'll still have my own little commemoration on March the seventh. I think of it often—not just that day, but all the days of the movement. . . . I'm just so happy that I could be a part of a thing that touched our souls. . . . We were just people, ordinary people, and we did it," Shey said.

The civil rights movement continued throughout the late 1960s and the 1970s. At the same time, changes were happening in other aspects of American life. The Vietnam War was escalating, as were the antiwar protests. Young people were at the center of the demonstrations against the war. Some young people, who were called "hippies," created a counterculture.

Corrina Laszlo's parents were hippies and she grew up on a commune in southern Colorado. "We had communal toothbrushes and two-seater outhouses. . . . The other children had names such as Star, Dipper, and Lump," Corrina said. She was free to climb cliffs and explore valleys. When she was six years old, her family moved to Santa Fe and Corrina realized she was different. For one thing, her mother sent her to school with concoctions of tofu, seaweed, and other health food while her classmates had bologna and cheese sandwiches. "I had no idea what a hippie was until I made the attempt to enter the mainstream and began to deal with stereotypes and prejudices," Corrina recalled.

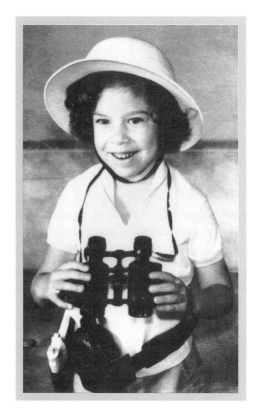 

Ellen Ochoa grew up in a time of unprecedented possibilities. As a young girl, she was photographed with her birthday presents. As a young woman, she was photographed as an astronaut.

Music was a central part of the counterculture, including folk music that typically pointed out the injustice and hypocrisy in society. Also during this time, an English rock-music group, The Beatles, burst onto the music scene and inspired many young musicians to start their own bands. Young women musicians, however, were not usually included.

"I really think that had to do with the roles that were put forward of what girls do and boys do," explained Holly Near, who became a well-known folksinger and songwriter. "All the kids started putting together bands. Everybody wanted to be in a band, everybody wanted to play the guitar. Well, the 'everybody' were boys. And I played the acoustic guitar, probably knew more chords and more about music than any of the guys who were diving in and plugging in their guitars. And it never even occurred to me to plug in. It's not even that I was told not to, it just didn't even cross my mind. . . . It just wasn't something girls did. So I put the guitar away and became a girl singer."

During this time, a new movement for women's equality started to grow. In 1963, two events happened that helped launch it. The Presidential Commission on the Status of Women, the first ever appointed, released a report that documented the difficulties and discrimination that

Three girls celebrating women's history.

women faced. Betty Friedan published *The Feminine Mystique,* in which she criticized the idea that marriage and motherhood were all that women needed to lead fulfilling lives.

Throughout the 1960s and '70s, gender roles were hotly debated. Nancy Kates's mother wanted her "to be perfectly feminine, an idealized little girl in pink dresses and patent leathers. . . . As a child, I guess I would have been a tomboy, given my druthers. Instead, when I was about five years old, my mother mysteriously transformed herself into a special agent from what I later called the 'Gender Police.' "

Catherine Anne Morgan, the author's sister, called Cam, grew up during the 1960s.

Nancy grew up in Boston, Massachusetts, and she can "still remember the day it all began. She went into my closet and removed my two pairs of dark blue corduroy pants, saying I was a 'big girl now,' and that, once they reached a certain age, girls didn't wear pants. She was very firm, almost severe, and somehow, even at five, I knew my mother was giving an opinion, but not necessarily telling the truth. I also remember having the sinking feeling that something was about to go terribly wrong. It was 1967, after all. Lots of women were wearing all sorts of clothes, including pants, and other unacceptably 'male' attire. But from that day forward, until the age of fourteen, I wore pants only to go skiing (at least as far as my mother knew).

"My wardrobe soon became an enormous source of friction between us. We would go to the nearby mall, brand new circa 1968, and argue endlessly about what I was to wear. Most of what I selected wasn't 'feminine' enough to pass muster with Mom; the clothes she picked for me were far too frilly for my taste, with itchy lace, and silly bows that always got in the way. . . .

"More than anything, my childhood was filled with confusing mixed messages about being a girl. My mother wanted me to be an ultra-femme; my father seemed to expect that I would excel at seemingly masculine activities like school and business. The message was a common one, I think: girls were supposed to be proud of being female, yet understand their places in a world run by men. . . . My parents built him [my brother] a basketball court in our backyard when I was ten or eleven. He used it for a little while, then moved on to street hockey and other sports. I, who was dying to play basketball, was not even allowed to set foot on the court. Of course, I'd sneak out and use it every chance I got. Eventually, when I was in ninth grade, I summoned up all my courage and tried out for the basketball team. My peers—who had known me only as shy, overweight, and nerdy—were shocked that I actually made the team. I was ecstatic, just to play on the JV [Junior Varsity team]. No one knew about my secret life practicing in the backyard."

Jeannine DeLombard, however, grew up during this time having the opposite struggle with her mother. "I clearly recall the battles my mother and I would have over 'appropriate' clothing and toys," Jeannine said. "I wanted to wear pouffy pastel party dresses and Mary Janes every day of the week; she bought me corduroys and hiking boots. I routinely begged for—and was routinely denied—what I saw as the staples of girlhood: Barbies, a nurse kit, and Tinker Bell play makeup. Instead, I received entire clans of politically correct dolls (the Sunshine Family was white and the Happy Family was black, but their hair and facial features were the same). Even my literary heroes were wrong. I aspired to be just like clever, stylish Nancy Drew, whom my mother dismissed as prissy and dependent; she thought Laura Ingalls, the boisterous tomboy from the *Little House on the Prairie* TV series, a much better role model.

The cover of a Nancy Drew mystery published in 1966.

"I grew up in a home where gender roles were anything but strict, and breaking out of them was strictly encouraged. . . . Labor was divided in our household on the basis of ability as much as gender. It was my father who stayed home with me (he was a student at the time) while my mother went off to work as a teacher in the local elementary school. . . .

"By a strange twist of sociocultural fate, my mother and I were in a similar situation: both of us could have gotten much of what we wanted

In the 1970s, nontraditional day care centers were established.
There, boys could play with dolls and girls could use a hammer.

as children if we only had been born boys. In the fifties, my mother's affinity for masculine clothing and activities was considered unnatural; in the seventies, my desire for ultra-feminine toys and accessories was perceived much the same way. Listening to 'William Wants a Doll' on my *Free to Be You and Me* record, I understood that for a boy to plead for a baby doll was daring and original, while for a girl to do so would be old-fashioned and unimaginative. I have no doubt that, had I been born a boy, my parents would have tried to interest me in tea sets and Betty Crocker ovens in an effort to steer me away from G.I. Joes and Hot Wheels. Dominated by a new kind of double standard, my childhood taught me that avoiding gender roles can be every bit as frustrating, limiting, and ridiculous as adhering to them."

As the women's movement gained momentum, new organizations

were formed to fight for equality, including the National Organization for Women (NOW). The words "feminism" and "feminist," which had been used during the first part of the century, reappeared. In 1913, Rebecca West, British novelist and critic, wrote, "I have never been able to find out precisely what feminism is: I only know that people call me a feminist whenever I express sentiments that differentiate me from a door-mat." The word "Ms." was introduced as an alternative to "Miss" or "Mrs.," the traditional forms of address that indicated a woman's mari-

A rally against rape.

tal status. New words were coined such as "sexism" and "women's liberation." Alice Walker, an American novelist, introduced the word "womanist" and defined it as "a black feminist or feminist of color. From the black folk expression that mothers say to female children, 'You acting womanish,' i.e., like a woman. . . . Responsible. In charge."

Many girls grew up with mothers who participated in the fight for equality. "Like most of my friends, I lived in a female-headed household," recalled Danzy Senna, who grew up in Boston, Massachusetts. "My mother raised us with the help of other women, a series of sidekick moms who moved in and out of our lives. In the evenings, we all converged in the kitchen, an orange-painted room on the second floor of our house. In the kitchen, laughter, food, and talk formed a safe space of women and children.

"I remember one dusky evening in particular, when a group of women from the local food cooperative came banging on our door. They wanted my mother's support in a march protesting violence against women. She liked these tough, working-class women and what they stood for, so while other mothers called their kids into dinner, ours dragged us into the streets. My sister, brother, and I were mortified as we ran alongside the march, giggling and pointing at the marching women [who were] chanting 'Women Unite—Take Back the Night!' The throngs were letting it all hang out: their breasts hung low, their leg hairs grew wild, their thighs were wide in their faded blue jeans. Some of them donned Earth shoes and T-shirts with slogans like 'A Women Needs a Man Like a Fish Needs a Bicycle.' [They] weren't in the least bit ashamed."

During the 1970s, Congress passed the Equal Rights Amendment (ERA), which read, "Equality of rights under the law shall not be denied or abridged by the United States or by any State on account of sex." If

Two girls participating in a march in 1977 in New York City.

thirty-eight states ratified it by June 30, 1982, the ERA would become the law of the land. When Kristin Lems was growing up, she and her mother worked to get the ERA ratified. Kristin grew up to be a songwriter and wrote a song called "My Mom's a Feminist." Some of the lyrics are:

> I was raised on equal rights, and furthermore
> She helped me see that equality is a goal worth fighting for.

By the mid-1970s, however, groups were organized to stop the women's movement because it was seen as a threat to the traditional family. In particular, the groups targeted the ERA and launched a fierce attack that included telling people that the ERA would mean unisex toilets and women in combat. When the deadline arrived on June 30, 1982, the ERA was defeated, three states short of passage. Sarah Morgan was nine years old at the time and did not pay much attention. However, a few years later she remembers reading a picture caption that told about the defeat of the ERA. "I was shocked," Sarah recalled. "I said 'What!' I had to reread it several times before I could really believe it. I could not understand why anyone would be against equal rights for women."

Although the ERA was defeated, the women's movement had brought about many changes. There were new laws, including ones that banned sex discrimination in employment and credit. The U.S. Supreme Court handed down a controversial ruling that protected a woman's right to choose

It took a lawsuit, but finally girls were allowed to participate in Little League.
This catcher and batter are attending the first tryouts in 1974.

to end a pregnancy. New opportunities had opened up, including the right of girls to play Little League baseball. "By the time I was born . . . things had changed a whole lot," says fourteen-year-old Elizabeth Jenkins-Sahlin. "That is thanks to the many women who devoted their lives to getting women's rights, among them Elizabeth Cady Stanton, my great-great-great-grandmother." According to Elizabeth, "In 1989, when my mother ran for elected office . . . she made me her 'campaign manager.' Even though I was only four years old then, I drove around with mom, helping her distribute campaign fliers. Mom won the election and is now an official in the legislative body. . . . She is one of many thousands of women today who do something about laws that affect women as well as men."

Take our Daughters To Work® Day began in 1993 as a way to introduce girls to the working world. In 1995, these girls spent the day with a chemist.

Girls growing up in America at the end of the twentieth century were more diverse than ever before as new immigrant girls came by land, sea, and air. The last wave of immigrant girls, who had come during the period between 1870 and World War I, came primarily from southern and eastern Europe. But with changes in the immigration law in 1965 that ended certain restrictions, girls started coming from many new countries, including Mexico, the Philippines, China and Hong Kong, Cuba, Vietnam, and India. Between 1991 and 1995, nearly 13,000 immigrants from 123 countries moved into Elmhurst, Queens, a section of New York City.

Yana Shteyn came to the United States from Odessa, Ukraine, part of the former Soviet Union, where she had trained for five years in a sport school in a special class for table tennis. According to Yana, "When I was thirteen my life completely changed because I came to the United States to the small city of Jacksonville, Florida, where table tennis is Ping-Pong, a fun game." Yana traveled to other cities where she could compete in tournaments and started winning. Before long, she was the number-one girl table tennis player in Florida.

QiQi Cheng arrived in 1996 from Shanghai, China. She was fifteen years old and knew only a few words of English. Three years later, she graduated from high school as valedictorian. Mirela Miraj came from Albania when she was fifteen years old. She and her family had been persecuted for their religious beliefs. "I have seen people who have suffered every atrocity and have still been able to survive and go on," Mirela says.

As the twenty-first century begins, girls have unprecedented possibilities. Nevertheless, girls still have to deal with a variety of gender role expectations that can limit their freedom. Growing numbers of girls, however, are determined not to be limited. "When I got my first skateboard I was probably around 12 years old," Ramdasha Bikceem explains. "It didn't really occur to me at the moment that what I was doing was considered out of the ordinary for a lot of girls. But as I got older and started getting more into skateboarding, I realized what role most girls played. . . . Their role was to sit on the sidewalk while the rest of the boys were havin' a rippin' time. At first I tried to ignore it and I even looked down upon these girls for not trying. . . . Now . . . I can only hope that they will see me there and hopefully see themselves one day. Or at least question what they're doing there sitting on the sidelines."

A young competitor in the 1976 U.S. skateboard competition. It was the first time that females were allowed to compete.

Kimberly Hatter from Houston, Texas, talks about how she became a rapper. "My rap career began when I was in the fifth grade and was met by extreme disapproval from my parents. They considered rap specifically . . . for MALES. They would have preferred for me to become a gospel singer. . . . My brothers, cousins, other family members, and friends strongly supported the idea of me becoming a female rapper. I was always the only female in a large group of boys rapping and beat boxing. . . . My greatest hope is to be an inspiration to other females who wish to defy the limitations and stereotypes placed on their lives by society."

Tammy Sue Lowe, who is a Cherokee Indian from Anderson, Missouri, plans on growing up to become the president of the United States. "Most people, upon finding out that I am female and minority, usually laugh when I tell them what I want to be. If they don't laugh, they tell me how unhonest politicians are. I want to change all of that."

In addition to gender role expectations, contemporary girls deal with a variety of complex issues. At every stage of their growing up, girls are bombarded with constantly changing images and definitions of beauty, acceptance, responsibility, and success. Many girls have to protect themselves from sexual harassment, abuse, and violence. Statistics compiled in 1999 illustrate what girls face. For example, eighth grade girls are more likely to use inhalants than boys their age; one in five ninth grade girls is currently sexually active; in the twelve-to-seventeen age group, nearly twenty percent of girls smoke cigarettes and nearly twenty percent drink alcohol; three out of five ninth to twelfth grade girls go on diets to lose weight; and twice as many girls as boys attempt suicide.

At this point in history, however, girls have something to help them that previous generations of girls could not even imagine—direct access to extraordinary amounts of information, advice, and support through the use of computers and the Internet. Some of the growing numbers of Web sites for girls include Purple Moon, A Girl's World, Girl Tech, and Girl Power. Millions of girls from around the world visit these sites each month. They can get answers to questions and do research on a variety of topics, including sexuality, eating disorders, and substance abuse. Girls also use the Internet to send messages to each other, write stories, and express their opinions. In GirlSpeak on the Web site, Girl Power, Stephanie wrote: "Every girl is unique in her own way. It doesn't matter what color we are, our shape, size, or the way we dress." Chloe, age 10, wrote: "Be yourself. Cool down when you're mad. Help people. Let other people help you. Be proud you're a girl. Don't give up girl power."

Elizabeth Murray is an inspiring example of girl power. She was born in 1981 and grew up in the Bedford Park section of the Bronx, New York. Her father was addicted to drugs and had AIDS. Her mother died of AIDS. Elizabeth says, "I was poor, lived in a rundown neighborhood and was neglected, left to raise myself." She lived in one apartment, then

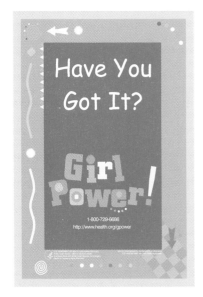

Girl Power! has become a popular slogan.

Some of the girls who serve on the editorial board of New Moon™: The Magazine for Girls and Their Dreams. *They select and edit material submitted by girls worldwide, as well as material by professional adult writers.*

another, and then on park benches and the streets. But she stayed in school and did her homework. In 1999, she graduated at the top of her class. Out of three thousand applicants, Elizabeth was one of six students to receive a major four-year scholarship awarded by the *New York Times* to students who had excelled in the face of formidable obstacles. She has applied to Harvard and Brown—two colleges that did not accept women until late in the twentieth century. When she was homeless, says Elizabeth, "I started to grasp the value of the lessons I was learning living on the streets. I knew, after overcoming these obstacles, next to nothing could hold me down."

Throughout American history, countless numbers of girls have overcome obstacles. They have made a difference. They have left a legacy. As the twenty-first century unfolds, future generations of girls will undoubtedly make their mark on American society, too.

Selected Sources for Further Reading

I consulted hundreds of primary and secondary sources in writing a history of growing up female in America. The following is a selected list of my sources for further reading:

Bolden, Tonya, ed. *33 things every girl should know*. New York: Crown, 1998.

Brumberg, Joan Jacobs. *The Body Project: An Intimate History of American Girls*. New York: Random House, 1997.

Carlip, Hillary. *Girl Power: Young Women Speak Out!* New York: Warner Books, 1995.

Carroll, Rebecca. *Sugar in the Raw: Voices of Young Black Girls in America*. New York: Crown, 1997.

Child, Lydia Maria. *The Girl's Own Book*. 1834. Reprint. Old Sturbridge Village, MA: Applewood Books, n.d.

Douglas, Susan J. *Where the Girls Are: Growing Up Female with the Mass Media*. New York: Random House, 1994.

Dubois, Ellen Carol and Vicki L. Ruiz. *Unequal Sisters*. New York: Routledge, 1990.

Earle, Alice Morse. *Child Life in Colonial Days*. 1899. Reprint. Williamstown, MA: Corner House Publishers, 1975.

Evans, Sara M. *Born for Liberty*. New York: The Free Press, 1997.

Fairbanks, Evelyn. *Days of Rondo: A Warm Reminiscence of St. Paul's Thriving Black Community in the 1930s and 1940s*. St. Paul, MN: Minnesota Historical Society Press, 1990.

Faust, Drew Gilpin. *Mothers of Invention*. New York: Vintage Books, 1996.

Franklin, Penelope, ed. *Private Pages: Diaries of American Women 1830s–1970s*. New York: Ballantine Books, 1986.

Gaar, Gillian G. *She's a Rebel: The History of Women in Rock & Roll*. Seattle: Seal Press, 1992.

Gilman, Carolyn and Mary Jane Schneider. *"The Way to Independence." Memories of a Hidatsa Indian Family 1840–1920*. St. Paul, MN: Minnesota Historical Society Press, 1987.

Gray, Heather M. and Samantha Phillips. *Real girl/real world*. Seattle: Seal Press, 1998.

Harvey, Brett. *The Fifties: A Women's Oral Guide*. New York: HarperCollins, 1993.

Havens, Catherine Elizabeth. *Diary of a Young Girl in Old New York*. New York: Henry Collins Brown, 1920.

Hine, Darlene Clark and Kathleen Thompson. *A Shining Thread of Hope: A History of Black Women in America*. New York: Broadway Books, 1998.

Hong, Maria, ed. *Growing Up Asian American*. New York: Avon Books, 1993.

Hurmence, Belinda, ed. *My Folks Don't Want Me to Talk about Slavery*. Winston-Salem, NC: John F. Blair Publishers, 1997.

Jacobs, Harriet A. *Incidents in the Life of a Slave Girl: Written by Herself*. Edited and with an introduction by Jean Fagan Yellin. Cambridge, MA: Harvard University Press, 1987.

Johnson, Dorothy M. *When You and I Were Young Whitefish*. Helena, MT: Montana Historical Society, 1997.

Jordon, Teresa. *Cowgirls: Women of the American West*. Lincoln, NE: University of Nebraska Press, 1992.

Katz, Jane, ed. *Messengers of the Wind: Native American Women Tell Their Life Stories*. New York: Ballantine Books, 1995.

Kerber, Linda. *Women of the Republic: Intellect and Ideology in Revolutionary America*. Chapel Hill: University of North Carolina Press, 1980.

Larcom, Lucy. *A New England Girlhood Outlined from Memory*. Boston: Houghton Mifflin, 1889.

Lee, Mary Paik. Edited with an introduction by Sucheng Chan. *Quiet Odyssey: A Pioneer Korean Woman in America*. Seattle: University of Washington Press, 1990.

Leonard, Eugenia Andruss. *The Dear-Bought Liberty*. Philadelphia: University of Pennsylvania Press, 1965.

Lerner, Gerda, ed. *The Female Experience: An American Documentary*. New York: Oxford University Press, 1992.

Marten, James. *Children of the Civil War*. Carbondale, IL: Southern Illinois University Press, 1998.

Miedzian, Myriam and Alisa Malinovich. *Generations: A Century of Women Speak About Their Lives*. New York: Atlantic Monthly Press, 1997.

Moynihan, Ruth Barnes, Cynthia Russett and Laurie Crumpacker. *Second to None: A Documentary History of American Women*. 2 vols. Lincoln: University of Nebraska Press, 1993.

Murphy, Virginia Reed. *Across the Plains in the Donner Party*. 1891. Reprint. Golden, CO: Outbooks, 1980.

Niethammer, Carolyn. *Daughters of the Earth: The Lives and Legends of American Indian Women*. New York: Simon & Schuster, 1977.

Norton, Mary Beth. *Founding Mothers and Fathers: Gendered Power and the Forming of American Society*. New York: Alfred A. Knopf, 1996.

Proper, David R. *Lucy Terry Prince: Singer of History*. Deerfield, MA: Pocumtuck Valley Memorial Association & Historic Deerfield, Inc., 1997.

Reinier, Jacqueline S. *From Virtue to Character: American Childhood, 1775–1850*. New York: Twayne Publishers, 1996.

Richards, Caroline Cowles. *Village Life in America*. New York: Henry Holt & Co., 1913.

Robbins, Trina. *A Century of Women Cartoonists*. Northampton, MA: Kitchen Sink Press, 1993.

Robinson, Harriet Hanson. *Loom and Spindle.* 1898. Reprint. Kailua, HI: Press Pacifica, 1976.

Ruiz, Vicki L. *From Out of the Shadows: Mexican Women in Twentieth Century America.* New York: Oxford University Press, 1998.

Shaw, Anna Howard. *The Story of a Pioneer.* New York: Harper & Brothers, 1915.

Sherr, Lynn. *Failure Is Impossible: Susan B. Anthony in Her Own Words.* New York: Times Books, 1995.

Simon, Kate. *Bronx Primitive: Portraits in a Childhood.* New York: The Viking Press, 1982.

Singer, Bennett L., ed. *Growing Up Gay/Growing Up Lesbian: A Literary Anthology.* New York: New Press, 1994.

Stanton, Elizabeth Cady. *Eighty Years & More: Reminiscences 1815–1897.* 1898. Reprint. New York: Schocken, 1971.

Sterling, Dorothy. *We Are Your Sisters: Black Women in the Nineteenth Century.* New York: Norton, 1984.

Taylor, Susie King. Edited by Patricia W. Romero and Willie Le Rose. *A Black Woman's Civil War Memoirs.* New York: Markus Wiener Publishing, 1988.

Ulrich, Laurel Thatcher. *A Midwife's Tale: The Life of Martha Ballard, Based on Her Diary, 1785–1812.* New York: Vintage Books, 1991.

Walker, Rebecca. *To Be Real.* New York: Anchor Books, 1995.

Washington, Margaret, ed. *Narrative of Sojourner Truth.* New York: Vintage, 1993.

Weatherford, Doris. *Milestones: A Chronology of American Women's History.* New York: Facts on File, 1997.

Webb, Sheyann and Rachel West Nelson as told to Frank Sikora. *Selma, Lord, Selma.* University, AL: University of Alabama Press, 1980.

Werner, Emmy E. *Pioneer Children on the Journey West.* Boulder, CO: Westview Press, 1995.

West, Elliott. *Growing Up with the Country: Childhood on the Far Western Frontier.* Albuquerque, NM: University of New Mexico Press, 1991.

Whitney, Gae Canfield. *Sarah Winnemucca of the Northern Paiutes.* Norman, OK: University of Oklahoma Press, 1988.

Willard, Frances E. *How I Learned to Ride the Bicycle.* 1895. Reprint. Sunnyvale, CA: Fair Oaks Publishing, 1991.

Winslow, Anna Green. Introduction and Notes by Alice Morse Earle. *Diary of Anna Green Winslow: A Boston School Girl of 1771.* Boston: Houghton Mifflin, 1894.

Wong, Jade Snow. *Fifth Chinese Daughter.* New York: Harper & Brothers, 1945.

Yung, Judy. *Unbound Feet: A Social History of Chinese Women in San Francisco.* Berkeley: University of California Press, 1995.

Zitkala-Ša. *American Indian Stories.* Boston: Ginn, 1921.

_____. "Impressions of an Indian Childhood." *Atlantic Monthly,* Vol. 85, January, 1900.

_____. "The School Days of an Indian Girl." *Atlantic Monthly,* Vol. 86, February, 1900.

Index

Photo Credits

10: From Alice Earle Morse, ed., *Diary of Anna Green Winslow: A Boston School Girl of 1771*. Boston: Houghton Mifflin, 1894 frontispiece; 13: Sharlot Hall Museum Library/Archives, Prescott, Arizona; 15 (all) Library of Congress; 19: *Frank Leslie's Illustrated Newspaper* (March 30, 1889): 125; 20: Minnesota Historical Society; 22: Library of Congress; 24: Jim McMahon; **Cover,** 26: The New York Public Library, New York; 27: Trustees of The British Museum; 28: The Historical Society of Pennsylvania; 30: Courtesy American Antiquarian Society; 31: The South Carolina Historical Society; 34: Library of Congress; 35: Courtesy American Antiquarian Society; 37: Photograph by Penny Colman; 38: U.S. Dept of the Interior, National Park Service, Adams National Historical Park; 40: Library of Congress; 41: Courtesy of the National Archives, Washington, D.C.; 42: From Ethel Stanwood Bolton and Eva Johnson Coe, *American Sampler.* Boston: Massachusetts. Society of the Colonial Dames of America, 1921, plate xviii; 43: Courtesy of Wethersfield Historical Society; 45: From Dorothy Sterling, ed., *We Are Your Sisters: Black Women in the Nineteenth Century.* New York: W.W. Norton, 1984, 65; 47: Library of Congress; 50: Courtesy of Louise Minks; **Cover,** 53: From Alice Earle Morse, ed., *Diary of Anna Green Winslow: A Boston School Girl of 1771.* Boston: Houghton Mifflin, 1894, 1; 55: Photograph by Penny Colman; 56: From Richardson Wright, *Forgotten Women.* Philadelphia: J.B. Lippincott, 1928, frontispiece; 58: The Connecticut Historical Society, Hartford, Connecticut; 60: Litchfield Historical Society; 61: Courtesy The Metropolitan Museum of Art, New York; 62: From Eliza Southgate Bowne, *A Girl's Life Eighty Years Ago.* 1887; reprint, New York: Corner House Publishers, 1980, frontispiece; 64: The Elfreth's Alley Association, Inc.; 65: Litchfield Historical Society; 66: The Library Company of Philadelphia; 67: Society for the Preservation of New England Antiquities, gift of Nina Fletcher Little; 69: Photographic Archives, Harold B. Lee Library, Brigham Young University, Provo, Utah; 71: From Richardson Wright, *Forgotten Women.* Philadelphia: J.B. Lippincott, 1928, 200; **Cover,** 73: From Mrs. L. Maria Child, *The Girl's Own Book.* 1834; reprint, Chester, CT: Applewood Books, n.d., 103; 74: University of Rochester; 75: University of Massachusetts, Lowell, Center for Lowell History; 77: American Museum of Textile History; 80: From Emmy E. Werner, *Pioneer Children on the Journey West.* Boulder: Westview Press, 1995; 81: Courtesy Solomon D. Butcher Collection, Nebraska State Historical Society; 83: "On the Way to the Summit" by William Gilbert Gaul. Oakland Museum of Art; 84: Courtesy Sutter's Fort State Historical Park, California Department of Parks and Recreation; 85: Nevada State Historical Society; 87: Library of Congress; 88 (right and left): Courtesy American Antiquarian Society; 90: Library of Congress; 91: Courtesy Solomon D. Butcher Collection, Nebraska State Historical Society; 93: California Department of Parks and Recreation; 94: Library of Congress; 96: Library of Congress; 98: From Carolyn Cowles Richards, *Village Life in America.* New York: Henry Holt, 1913, frontispiece; **Cover,** 99: Collection of Ontario County Historical Society, Canandaigua, New York; 101: Cape Fear Historical Society, Wilmington, North Carolina; 103: © 1988 by the Ulysses S. Grant Association. Reprinted with permission of the publisher Southern Illinois University Press; 104: Penn School Papers, Southern Historical Collection, University of North Carolina; **Cover,** 106: Courtesy Museum of New Mexico, Neg. No. 137333; **Cover,** 107: Library of Congress; 109: Courtesy American Antiquarian Society; 110: University of New Hampshire Library, Special Collections; 112: Frances E. Willard Museum; 113: State Historical Society of Iowa; **Cover,** 114: Collection of the Paterson Museum; 115: University of Illinois at Chicago, The University Library, Special Collection; **Cover,** 116: Collection of Immigrant City Archives, Lawrence, Massachusetts; 117: Courtesy of Museum of New Mexico, Neg. No. 1035; 118: Library of Congress; **Cover,** 119: Library of Congress; **Cover,** 120: Library of Congress; 121 (top): Courtesy Solomon D. Butcher Collection, Nebraska State Historical Society; **Cover,** 121 (bottom): National Women's Hall of Fame; 124: Library of Congress; **Cover,** 126: Courtesy Colorado Historical Society; **Cover,** 127 (top, left, bottom right): Library of Congress; 128 (left and right): Collection of the author; **Cover,** 129: Library of Congress; 130: Library of Congress; 131: Sharlot Hall Museum Library/Archives, Prescott, Arizona; 132: Library of Congress; **Cover,** 133: Minnesota Historical Society; 134 From Teresa Jordan, *Cowgirls: Women of the American West.* Lincoln, NE: University of Nebraska Press, 217; 135: Chicano Research Collection, Arizona State University Libraries; 137: Library of Congress; **Cover,** 138: Sharlot Hall Museum Library/Archives, Prescott, Arizona; 139: Girl Scouts of the U.S.A.; 140: League of Women Voters;

Text Credits